Level I

Grades 4-5

Blue Ribbon Spelling and Vocabulary

For Kids Who Always Get 100 on the Friday Test

Catherine Slough Valentino

DALE SEYMOUR PUBLICATIONS

Illustrations: Dennis Nolan
Cover design: John Edeen

Order number DS03401
ISBN 0-86651-196-2

DALE
SEYMOUR
PUBLICATIONS
P.O. BOX 10888
PALO ALTO, CA 94303

2 3 4 5 6 7 8 9 10 11-MA-95 94 93 92 91

Preface

One of the most frustrating problems in teaching spelling to a heterogeneous group of elementary and junior high school students is the wide range of individual differences that a teacher encounters. In most classrooms, the students range over four to five ability levels in all skill areas. Teachers generally try to individualize reading and math instruction to address these student needs. It is not uncommon to find, for example, three reading groups and two math groups at any grade from K to 6 (although in junior high, students are often grouped homogeneously in English and math).

In the peripheral language arts, such attempts at individualization are practically nonexistent. Very few classrooms have more than one spelling group. Publishers of spelling programs are thus under great pressure to address student differences within a single text.

Most programs *do* include enrichment and challenge words in the student text, as well as remedial activities for less able students. Teacher editions include even more suggestions. But there is a problem with this approach: in practice, all the students in a given class go through the entire weekly series of activities, then are assigned remedial or enrichment activities *in addition* to the regular work. Rare is the teacher who administers a spelling pretest on Monday and then regroups according to student performance. Teachers who do use the extra activities specifically to meet individual needs are usually focusing on the remedial child rather than the talented one.

A single enrichment activity tacked onto an inappropriate daily program will *not* address the needs of academically talented students. Reacting to the plight of the child who must endure work that is 90 percent review year after year, parents have begun to lobby for appropriate classroom work for their gifted and talented youngsters. They have been joined by leaders in gifted education who have long espoused a differentiated curriculum that addresses the basic diet of these children.

I designed the *Blue Ribbon* activities to provide classroom teachers with a complete supplementary spelling program for their above-average students. For ease of use, the *Blue Ribbon* lessons can be tied directly to the same skills and principles covered by your basal spelling program. However, these lessons introduce the better students to more sophisticated vocabulary words. They also offer spelling activities that stress *thinking skills* in addition to the exploration and manipulation of written words. The *Blue Ribbon* program provides able students with a standard Monday-through-Friday format that produces capable, independent learners.

I have made every effort to offer teachers a program that is highly motivating, challenging, and flexible. *Blue Ribbon Spelling and Vocabulary* places the responsibility for follow-through and vertical progress where it belongs—with the academically talented student.

Catherine Valentino

Introduction

Level I of *Blue Ribbon Spelling and Vocabulary* is designed for use with academically talented students in grades 4 and 5. It can also serve as a supplementary program for average 6th-grade students.

The sequence of spelling skills closely parallels that of major spelling programs. Blue Ribbon spelling words, however, are significantly more difficult. This allows any teacher to individualize the regular program for students who are able to handle a more sophisticated spelling and writing vocabulary.

Using the Worksheets

Each *Blue Ribbon* lesson is divided into four numbered parts, appearing on two reproducible worksheet pages. These can be used in a four-day sequence, followed by the standard weekly spelling test on Friday.

The Blue Ribbon words for study are introduced on Monday in Part 1 of each lesson. Students are expected to read, write, define, and study each of five new words, which are to be committed to memory. Parts 2, 3, and 4 of each lesson are to be completed on Tuesday, Wednesday, and Thursday—or according to your own preferred schedule. You may want to give advanced students the entire week's work on Monday and make them responsible for pacing their spelling and vocabulary study throughout the week.

On Friday, while the rest of the class is tested on the standard wordlist, students in this program must use each of the Blue Ribbon words in a complete and properly spelled sentence. If the program is being used in a gifted resource-room setting, the same procedure will work, or the teacher may dictate the words aloud. Some classroom teachers may want to dictate the words to "Blue Ribbon" students at the end of the standard list. This gives advanced students a review of the standard wordlist while also checking their Blue Ribbon work.

The program is designed to challenge your talented students, and they are not expected to get 100 percent on every activity. On the other hand, the program is not merely an "enrichment" program in the usual sense of the word. It is intended as a basic supplement to your regular classroom spelling program, and participating students should be held accountable for completing the lessons as assigned.

Using Review Lessons

Every sixth two-page lesson is an optional review, with a wordlist comprised of the Blue Ribbon words from the previous five lessons. Along with each review wordlist, there appears a collection of ten all-purpose activities. These are designed to be used flexibly with students who need to review either the spelling or the meaning of the Blue Ribbon words.

A variety of different review exercises have been suggested to stimulate student interest, including story and poem writing, word search puzzles, word games, and dictionary research. However, students should not be expected to complete more than *three* activities for any given review lesson. You may want to assign specific activities as a formal part of the program, or you might allow students to select those activities that appeal most to them.

About the Blue Ribbon Words

Each Blue Ribbon lesson is developed around a single unifying theme. The topics are drawn from general areas of student interest, from the Wild West to outer space, as well as from the curricular areas of science, social studies, and mathematics. Through this thematic approach, spelling and vocabulary development are integrated with the students' writing and other class activities. This process forestalls the problems that arise when spelling and vocabulary are taught in isolation.

With the exception of the five Blue Ribbon words in each lesson, which must be mastered, the remainder of the vocabulary words that appear in each lesson serve simply to reinforce general spelling principles and to introduce more difficult words that students may be seeing in their recreational and developmental reading.

Blue Ribbon Lessons

Don't Be a Litterbug

1

General principle   The sounds /a/ and /e/ are usually spelled **a** and **e**.

Read the paragraphs below. Your Blue Ribbon words are underlined.

One day on the school bus, Abe Picketupp saw Ima Slawb toss an empty can out the bus window and down an <u>embankment</u>.

"Stop the bus!" shouted Abe. "Ima just littered our environment with <u>malice</u> aforethought."

"That's not true," retorted Ima <u>candidly</u>. "It was just an insignificant old can."

"Ima," the bus driver admonished, "an animal's <u>habitat</u> can be destroyed by your thoughtless littering. I'm giving you <u>ample</u> warning. One more can out the window, and I'll have one less rider on this bus."

1. Write your Blue Ribbon words on a sheet of paper.
2. Using a dictionary, write each word's phonetic spelling and definition. Then write each word in a new sentence.
3. Learn the spelling and definition of each Blue Ribbon word. Be prepared to write each word, properly spelled, in a complete sentence.

2

Abe Picketupp found the objects below discarded beside the roadway. Identify or define each one. Mark any vowel that has the sound of /a/ or /e/.

1. a scrap of parchment _____
2. a fragment of insulation _____
3. a plastic receptacle _____
4. a pamphlet about asbestos _____
5. a bent spatula _____

short a and e   **1**

3

One day a police officer heard the following excuses for littering in a park.

"I was distracted by a tarantula on my path and I accidentally dropped my trash."

"An orangutan stalked along behind me, scattering debris."

"I was just conducting an experiment. I was attempting to see how effective law enforcement agencies are in apprehending litterers. I now know they are very good at it."

Define the following words that were used in the excuses. Mark any vowels that have the sound /a/ or /e/.

1. tarantula _____

2. orangutan _____

3. stalked _____

4. scattering _____

5. debris _____

6. enforcement _____

7. agencies _____

8. apprehending _____

4

All the litterbugs who were apprehended were sentenced to do this activity in order to avoid a hefty fine.

Make at least 25 words that contain the /e/ sound, using the letters in this sentence: **Litter is everyone's problem.**

How many words can you make?

_____ _____ _____
_____ _____ _____
_____ _____ _____
_____ _____ _____
_____ _____ _____
_____ _____ _____
_____ _____ _____
_____ _____

The Hot Potato Test

1

General principle   The sounds /i/, /o/, and /u/ are usually spelled **i, o,** and **u.**

Read the paragraph below. Your Blue Ribbon words are underlined.

    Mr. Yellhizhedoff, a fourth-grade teacher, presented a <u>ponderous</u> problem to the class. "In this closed shoebox with holes in the top, there may or may not be a hot baked potato," he <u>intimated</u>. "It is your <u>responsibility</u> to determine the presence or absence of the spud without touching the box. Devise any tests or experiments you choose that will <u>disclose</u> the tuber. Any <u>illogical</u> tests should be discarded."

1. Write your Blue Ribbon words on a sheet of paper.
2. Using a dictionary, write each word's phonetic spelling and definition. Then write each word in a new sentence.
3. Learn the spelling and definition of each Blue Ribbon word. Be prepared to write each word, properly spelled, in a complete sentence.

2

Devise a test to disclose the presence or absence of the hot baked potato in the closed shoebox. Describe your test in complete sentences. Identify any words containing the sounds /a/, /e/, /i/, /o/, or /u/ by placing a short-vowel mark over the appropriate vowels.

short i, o, and u   **3**

3

This word search contains more than 20 words that describe or are associated with heat. Circle as many as you can, then write them in a list. The hidden words read either straight across or straight down.

```
A A B U R N M K L A D F U I L O T
C D O H O T B C E S B S C A L D O
F F S R K L C A N H J I G N I T E
L K F E W Q I N F E R N O M T B C
A I E S A T N O M S E G O T E S O
M E D C O M D E F J K E L I M M M
I E M O L T E N A B E D P N P O B
N P E R O O R T M U S Q P C E L U
G A L C Y R S E A R I N G I R D S
P U T H Y R U I G N Z N O N A E T
E F E T U I M N M J Z L O E T R I
P O D D F A S A M L O R R U I B
E N E K F U E L U A I C H A R T L
Q U G H I O K L E C N H A T E A E
A S W E L T E R I N G I N E G L Y
```

4

Mr. Yellhizhedoff evaluated his students' hot-potato tests on Thursday afternoon. One student had invented a unique method for disclosing the potato. The following paragraphs describe what happened. Rewrite the sentences, filling in the missing letters.

"Ch__ldr__n," Mr. Y__llh__zh__d__ff announced, "I want to

see the t__sts you h__ve devised. St__p the ch__tter

__mmediately __nd l__t's g__t down to busin__ss. B__njam__n,

c__n you d__monstrate your m__thod to the cl__ss?"

"You b__t!" __nswered B__njam__n. He pl__pped a p__t of

b__tt__r on the t__p of the b__x.

"Good grief!" __xclaimed Mr. Y__llh__zh__d__ff. "__t's

m__lt__ng all over the l__d!"

short i, o, and u

What's for Dinner?

1

General principle The sounds /ā/ and /ē/ are sometimes spelled **a** and **e**.

Read the sentences below. Your Blue Ribbon words are underlined.

- Abraham discovered an <u>ingenious</u> method for feeding his meatloaf to the dog under the table.
- Amelia is <u>revitalized</u> every time she eats fried eggplant.
- A <u>savory</u> stew simmered away on the stove.
- Todd was <u>elated</u> to discover abalone on the menu.
- "No vegetables, no dessert," is a point that parents tend to <u>belabor</u>.

1. Write your Blue Ribbon words on a sheet of paper.
2. Using a dictionary, write each word's phonetic spelling and definition. Then write each word in a new sentence.
3. Learn the spelling and definition of each Blue Ribbon word. Be prepared to write each word, properly spelled, in a complete sentence.

2

You are sent to the store before dinner with this shopping list. In what section of the supermarket would you look for each item? The first one is located for you.

1. preserves ____jams & jellies____
2. abalone _____
3. okra _____
4. tripe _____
5. pumpernickel _____
6. eclairs _____
7. mangoes _____
8. artichokes _____
9. chives _____
10. basil _____
11. filet mignon _____
12. skate _____

Supermarket Sections

Bakery Goods
Beverages
Dairy
Fruits
Herbs & Spices
Housewares
Jams & Jellies
Meats
Seafood
Soups
Vegetables

long a and e 5

3

Your father needed each of these tools of the cooking trade when he prepared your dinner. Write a complete sentence to describe what he did with each item.

1. colander _____

2. spatula _____

3. baster _____

4. citrus juice extractor _____

5. condiments _____

6. garnishes _____

7. vegetable dicer _____

4

Your five-year-old cousin has taught herself to write phonetically. She sends you this recipe as a present. Translate the recipe to discover her favorite dessert. Rewrite it, spelling each word correctly.

Meye Phamus Apull Peye Resipee
Taik nyn phresh apulls and kuht thehm yntu litull pesez. Micks in suhm shoogur and suhm flouher and spysez. Pore thuh mickstyour yntu uh bocks uhf Ritz crakkurz. Shaik yt uhp. Emptea thuh bocks ynto uh peye pann. Baik yn uh 350° uhvin and surv yt waurm. Yt'z dielishus!

Meany Mouse Strikes Again

1

General principle   The sound /ī/ is often spelled **i** or **y**. The sound /ō/ is often spelled **o.**

Read the paragraphs below. Your Blue Ribbon words are underlined.

   Meany Mouse, the notorious criminal, terrorized the tiny village of Catbegone.

   "What atrocious behavior you have," a crowd of Catbegone citizens chided. "You will be forced to dodge projectiles if you don't cease at once, you little tyrant."

   "Don't trifle with me," bellowed Meany Mouse as he scurried toward the crowd.

   The citizens then proceeded to fling moldy grapes at the odious aggressor.

1. Write your Blue Ribbon words on a sheet of paper.
2. Using a dictionary, write each word's phonetic spelling and definition. Then write each word in a new sentence.
3. Learn the spelling and definition of each Blue Ribbon word. Be prepared to write each word, properly spelled, in a complete sentence.

2

Each of the words below is a synonym for a word in the story above. Match each numbered word with one from the story.

1. began _____

2. toss _____

3. frightened _____

4. roared _____

5. decayed _____

6. scampered _____

7. attacker _____

8. stop _____

long vowels with silent e   **7**

3

One day the citizens of Catbegone received word that Meany Mouse was planning a dastardly deed. They quickly passed a message from mouse hole to mouse hole. To prevent interception by Meany Mouse, they developed a secret code.

Translate and rewrite the message. Then answer the following question: How many /ō/ or /ī/ sounds are contained in the note? The first sentence has been started for you.

Mig hty/m ice/un ite! Ou rho meisgoi ngto beov errun. Gohi de unt ilth eco astis cle arandth e chi messtri kefi ve. Bea squi eta sam ouse.

Total number /ō/ _____

Total number /ī/ _____

4

Catbegone citizens have banned the use of any word beginning with the letters **c-a-t**. Complete the following words that are not a part of their vocabulary. Use your dictionary if you need to. Spelling counts!

1. A mail-order book   c a t __ __ __ __
2. A disaster   c a t __ __ __ __ __ __ __ __
3. A player on a baseball team   c a t __ __ __ __
4. The larva of a moth or butterfly   c a t __ __ __ __ __ __ __
5. Tomato sauce for french fries   c a t __ __ __
6. Bovine animals   c a t __ __ __
7. A short nap   c a t __ __ __

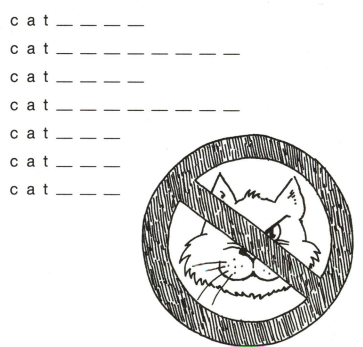

Bored Silly

1

General principle Some sounds are spelled with double consonants but are pronounced as a single consonant.

Read the paragraph below. Your Blue Ribbon words are underlined.

Boredom is a major <u>dilemma</u> for school children each August. Lying in a <u>hammock</u> with a good book is just not a twelve-year-old's idea of fun, at least not every day of the summer. <u>Haggling</u> with parents about mowing lawns and cleaning out closets isn't any fun either. Sometimes all you can do is sit and <u>twiddle</u> your thumbs. Who started all this <u>gibberish</u> about summer vacation anyway?

1. Write your Blue Ribbon words on a sheet of paper.
2. Using a dictionary, write each word's phonetic spelling and definition. Then write each word in a new sentence.
3. Learn the spelling and definition of each Blue Ribbon word. Be prepared to write each word, properly spelled, in a complete sentence.

2

One technique for overcoming boredom is learning to amuse yourself. After you complete this repetitious activity, however, you may be bored silly! Write the words with repeated consonants.

1. concealed   __ __ dd __ __
2. the highest point   __ __ mm __ __
3. oar   __ __ dd __ __
4. boastful person   __ __ __ gg __ __ __ __
5. less bright   __ __ mm __ __
6. panhandler   __ __ gg __ __
7. to drive insane   __ __ dd __ __
8. soaked through   __ __ gg __
9. round paving stone   __ __ bb __ __
10. eye protectors   __ __ gg __ __ __

3

Boredom affects everyone at one time or another. Scientists have studied boredom in human beings and have found two major causes. These causes are listed at the left side of the grid below. Four letters are listed across the top.

In each category, list one item that begins with the given letter. Each answer should name something that is boring to you. One is filled in for you.

Look up the words if you are unsure of their meanings. You will receive special commendation if your answers contain double consonants.

	m	d	b	g
inactivity				
repetition		**digging weeds**		

4

Can animals become bored? Why or why not? _____

_____

Write a short story describing a boring moment or experience in the life of an animal. Use each of these Blue Ribbon words: *dilemma, hammock, haggling, twiddle, gibberish.* Remember, spelling counts!

Example   Baby Boa Suffers from 'Boadom'

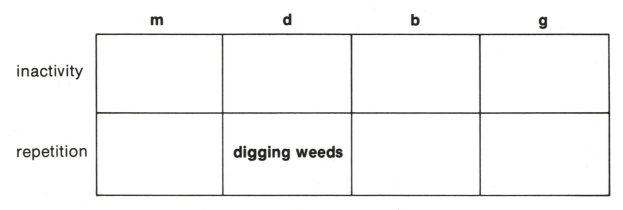

Blue Ribbon Review Lesson

Your Blue Ribbon Review Words

embankment, malice, candidly, habitat, ample

ponderous, intimated, responsibility, disclose, illogical

ingenious, revitalized, savory, elated, belabor

notorious, atrocious, tyrant, trifle, odious

dilemma, hammock, haggling, twiddle, gibberish

Review Activities

Use your Blue Ribbon review words to complete as many of the following activities as your teacher assigns.

1. Classify all of the Blue Ribbon words into three separate categories, based on their phonetic respellings or their meanings. You may select *any three categories,* but every word on the list must fit into one of them.

2. Use at least 20 of the Blue Ribbon words in a short story of no longer than 300 words. You may use up to five Blue Ribbon words in the title.

3. Use a word search grid to create your own word search puzzle. Your puzzle should contain at least 15 Blue Ribbon words.

4. Arrange the Blue Ribbon words in "backwards" alphabetical order. In other words, first look at the *last* letter of each word to determine alphabetical order, then at the next-to-last letter, and so forth.

5. From the Blue Ribbon word lists, select the five easiest and the five hardest words to spell. Arrange the five hardest words from most to least difficult. Arrange the five simplest words from easier to easiest. Write a sentence describing why your hardest word was difficult to spell and why your easiest word was a snap.

6. Find as many smaller words as you can in each Blue Ribbon word. You may *not* mix up the letters in the word. For example, the word *example* contains four smaller words: *exam, ample, am,* and *amp.*

7. Write one synonym and one antonym for 15 Blue Ribbon words. Make a chart like this to show your work:

Blue Ribbon word	Synonym	Antonym

8. Write a poem using at least ten Blue Ribbon words. You may want to experiment with a particular poetry form, such as haiku or a cinquain.

9. Change ten Blue Ribbon words into new words by changing no more than three letters in each word. For example, the word *elated* can be changed to the word *flared* by changing the first **e** to **f** and the **t** to **r.** Making nouns plural, changing verb endings, or changing the total number of letters in a word is strictly prohibited.

10. Some of the Blue Ribbon words have several meanings. Research the words in the list and write down a new, unusual, or obscure meaning for at least ten of them. Use each word in a complete sentence that illustrates the unusual meaning you found.

The Bermuda Triangle

1 — General principle

The vowel sounds /ā/ and /ō/ are often spelled with two letters. The sound /ā/ can be spelled **ai** and **ay.** The sound /ō/ can be spelled **oa** and **ow.**

Read the sentences below. Your Blue Ribbon words are underlined.

- Scientists have made many <u>inroads</u> into the mystery of the Bermuda Triangle.
- The new crew member timidly <u>broached</u> the topic of the Bermuda Triangle with the airplane's pilot before take-off.
- The sea water near the wreckage was <u>tainted</u> with the products of underwater decay.
- The vessel's cargo lay in <u>disarray</u> on the ocean floor.
- The sailor's ditty <u>foreshadowed</u> the sinking of his ship in the Bermuda Triangle.

1. Write your Blue Ribbon words on a sheet of paper.
2. Using a dictionary, write each word's phonetic spelling and definition. Then write each word in a new sentence.
3. Learn the spelling and definition of each Blue Ribbon word. Be prepared to write each word, properly spelled, in a complete sentence.

2

The Bermuda Triangle is an area in the ocean near the island of Bermuda. Some pilots and sailors claim that the area has the power to sink ships and planes. In this activity, the "Bermuda Triangle" can sink any ship or plane that surrounds a word with the vowel sound /ā/ or /ō/. Identify the doomed vessels by enclosing them in a triangle.

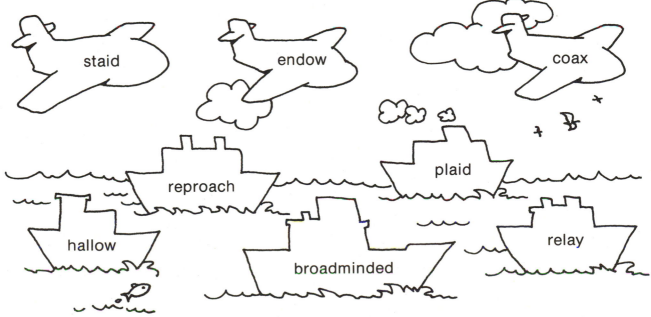

3

Some scientists argue that people's fears about the Bermuda Triangle are based on superstition, not fact. They point out that such fears are not logical. Consider this premise (a statement or belief):

Premise More than fifty ships and twenty aircraft have disappeared without explanation in the area called the Bermuda Triangle.

Write a sentence telling why each of the following statements *does not necessarily follow* from the premise.

1. The Bermuda Triangle is more dangerous to ships than planes.

_____

_____

2. It is safer to travel around the Bermuda Triangle than to travel through it.

_____

_____

3. A hot-air balloon will not sink in the Bermuda Triangle.

_____

_____

4

This yellowed and waterstained message was found sealed in a bottle floating off the coast of Bermuda. Complete the message by filling each blank with the letters **ai, ay, oa,** or **ow** as you copy the story.

My d____s are filled with the fell____ship of s____lors and the spr____ of waves lapping against the bow. The rem____ns of b____ts that have str____ed too close to the Bermuda Triangle fl____t sl____ly by. I will pr____se the d____ we are through these str____ts and the c____st of America is in sight.

Substitutes

1

General principle   Long vowel sounds are often spelled with two letters. Two ways to spell /ē/ are **ea** and **ee**.

Read the paragraphs below. Your Blue Ribbon words are underlined.

The remote-control toy car <u>careened</u> around the desks in Room 4 with its horn blaring. After the car ran into the substitute teacher, Mrs. Whymee, she began to <u>seethe</u>.

"I do not <u>deem</u> laughing the best thing to do in this situation," shouted Mrs. Whymee. "Don't try to <u>appease</u> me after this outburst, Room 4 students. I think that your school principal will consider this class's behavior a <u>breach</u> of responsibility."

1. Write your Blue Ribbon words on a sheet of paper.
2. Using a dictionary, write each word's phonetic spelling and definition. Then write each word in a new sentence.
3. Learn the spelling and definition of each Blue Ribbon word. Be prepared to write each word, properly spelled, in a complete sentence.

2

Copy the paragraph below, filling each blank with one of the following /ē/ words: *dealings, screeched, league, heed, demeanor, feats, peevish.*

"What's going on!" the principal _____ when she heard the clamor coming from Room 4. "_____ my words," she announced as she entered the noisy classroom. "I become quite _____ when I see a class with this kind of _____. I do not consider your _____ to be appropriate school behavior. I think you are all in _____ against your substitute, Mrs. Whymee. We will have no further _____ on this matter. Is that clear?"

3

After lunch, Mrs. Whymee divided the class into teams by giving one of the words below to each student. The students on Team I received words in which the letters **ea** had the /e/ sound. Team II students were given words that contained the /ē/ sound. Write the words of Team I and Team II.

death	plea	pheasant	dealt	steam
cheap	pleasant	yeast	creak	reteach
heavy	wealthy	preach	healthy	realm
please	defeat	sweat	leaden	meager

Team I /e/   Team II /ē/

_____ _____   _____ _____

_____ _____   _____ _____

_____ _____   _____ _____

_____ _____   _____ _____

_____ _____   _____ _____

4

The word *said* is one of the most overused words in the English language. Write as many substitutes as you can for the word *said*. Try to think of at least one substitute that begins with each letter of the alphabet, except **x** and **z**. You will receive one point for each correctly spelled substitution.

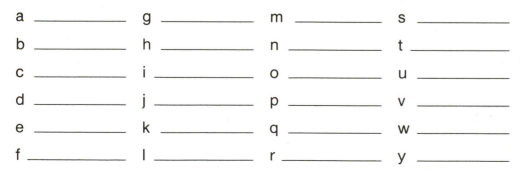

a _____   g _____   m _____   s _____

b _____   h _____   n _____   t _____

c _____   i _____   o _____   u _____

d _____   j _____   p _____   v _____

e _____   k _____   q _____   w _____

f _____   l _____   r _____   y _____

16 *ee and ea*

Never Cry Wolf

1

General principle The vowel sounds /ā/, /ī/, and /ō/ are often followed by a consonant and a silent **e: a__e, i__e,** and **o__e.**

Read the sentences below. Your Blue Ribbon words are underlined.

- It is very infantile to cry for help as a joke.
- If you have ever cried wolf, your chances of getting help when you really need it are remote.
- Be precise when reporting the location of an accident or an emergency.
- Do not agitate the guard dogs, because they are trained to attack.
- Someone should chastise the children for reporting a false-alarm fire.

1. Write your Blue Ribbon words on a sheet of paper.
2. Using a dictionary, write each word's phonetic spelling and definition. Then write each word in a new sentence.
3. Learn the spelling and definition of each Blue Ribbon word. Be prepared to write each word, properly spelled, in a complete sentence.

2

1. The most common English word used in an emergency is the word HELP. Is HELP the loudest word you could use to attract attention? Why or why not?

_____

_____

2. Compare long-vowel words with short-vowel words. Compare consonant sounds in words. Which sounds can be pronounced with more force? Why?

_____

_____

3. Choose a word to replace the word HELP in an emergency. Explain the reasons for your choice.

_____

_____

_____

_____

long vowels with silent e **17**

3

These verbs describe various sorts of human reactions in an emergency. Define each one. Mark every long vowel with a long-vowel mark.

1. to flee _____

2. to mobilize _____

3. to panic _____

4. to stampede _____

5. to bolt _____

6. to sacrifice _____

7. to donate _____

8. to respond _____

9. to ignore _____

10. to gape _____

4

Write a sentence telling how each of the items below might be used in an emergency. Be sure to describe the emergency situation you envision.

1. a taper _____

_____

2. a telescope _____

_____

3. a stake _____

_____

4. a spade _____

_____

5. twine _____

_____

Sound Off

1 | General principle

Two consonant letters together often stand for only one sound. The sound /n/ can be spelled **kn** or **gn**; the sound /r/ can be spelled **wr**; the sound /m/ can be spelled **mb.**

Read the paragraph below. Your Blue Ribbon words are underlined.

The sputtering sound arose from behind the grassy <u>knoll</u>, which was partially hidden by a chilling fog. The mist was <u>numbing</u> as the scouts clambered up the slippery hill to investigate. By the time they reached the top, their clothes were <u>wringing</u> wet. They threw their <u>knapsacks</u> down and peered over the small summit. At first the <u>gnarled</u> tree hid the source of the sound. Then, they saw it. . . .

1. Write your Blue Ribbon words on a sheet of paper.
2. Using a dictionary, write each word's phonetic spelling and definition. Then write each word in a new sentence.
3. Learn the spelling and definition of each Blue Ribbon word. Be prepared to write each word, properly spelled, in a complete sentence.

2 | Finish the short story above, using all five Blue Ribbon words.

3

Imitating natural sounds with words like *pow* or *bow-wow* is called *onomatopoeia* (on' ə mat' ə pē' ə).

Onomatopoeia often involves words with two or more consonant sounds together (blends), as in *sputter* and *clang.* Other "sound" words may stress a single consonant sound, as in *buzz* or *hum.* Still others, like *cock-a-doodle-doo,* repeat a syllable or sound to make a longer phrase.

List at least 18 onomatopoetic words that follow these three spelling patterns. Place each word in the proper column below.

Consonant blends	Stressed consonant sound	Repeated syllable or sound
sputter	buzz	bow wow

4

Sometimes the sounds made by inanimate objects are described by comparing them with human actions. This is called *personification,* which means making an object behave like or have the qualities of a person.

Fill in the following phrases with human-action verbs and adverbs to describe each object's sound.

1. The ocean _____ at the sailors.

2. The pines _____ near the tent.

3. The brook _____ to the picnickers.

4. The old gate _____ as it swung open.

5. The kettle _____ on the stove.

6. The wind _____ in my ears.

7. The foghorn _____ to the ships.

8. The rain _____ on the roof.

Bumper Stickers

1

General principle   Two consonants pronounced together are called a consonant blend. Some examples of consonant blends are **sk, sn, sm,** and **st.**

Read the paragraph below. Your Blue Ribbon words are underlined.

   The owner of the brand-new bumper sticker store, Smalltalk's, was skeptical that the store would be open before summer. There were just too many snags in getting the stickers printed. The first set of stickers delivered was smudged. The printing of the remaining stickers was postponed until the equipment was cleaned. The final obstacle in opening the store was the malfunctioning cash register.

1. Write your Blue Ribbon words on a sheet of paper.

2. Using a dictionary, write each word's phonetic spelling and definition. Then write each word in a new sentence.

3. Learn the spelling and definition of each Blue Ribbon word. Be prepared to write each word, properly spelled, in a complete sentence.

2

Ms. Smalltalk was elated when opening day finally arrived. She invited all the local business owners to her shop to celebrate the big day and presented each one with a personalized bumper sticker. The butcher, for example, received a sticker that said:

PLEASED TO MEAT YOU!

Design a bumper sticker for each of these guests.

1. the car dealer _____

2. the baker _____

3. the jeweler _____

4. the banker _____

5. the electrician _____

3

Alliteration is the repetition of the same beginning letter or sound in two or more words, such as "**s**uffering **s**uccotash." Ms. Smalltalk specializes in bumper stickers that use the technique of alliteration. For example: EVEN STRONG STALLIONS STUMBLE IN A STAMPEDE.

Write an alliterative bumper sticker for each of these consonant blends.

1. sm _____

2. sk _____

3. sn _____

4

Ms. Smalltalk's business expanded so rapidly that she was able to market a new line of products. Her new line, "Talking T-Shirts," featured humorous homonym-jokes such as "I'M WAISTING AWAY TO NOTHING" for people on a diet, and "TALKING ALOUD IS NOT ALLOWED" for a librarian.

Design three talking T-shirts and describe each intended customer. Be sure to use homonyms, the way Ms. Smalltalk did.

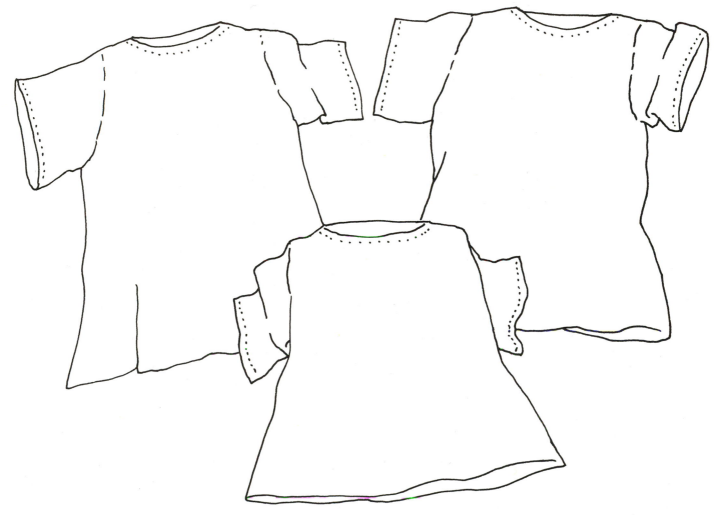

Blue Ribbon Review Lesson

Your Blue Ribbon Review Words

inroads, broached, tainted, disarray, foreshadowed

careened, seethe, deem, appease, breach

infantile, remote, precise, agitate, chastise

knoll, numbing, wringing, knapsacks, gnarled

skeptical, snags, smudged, postponed, obstacle

Review Activities
Use your Blue Ribbon review words to complete as many of the following activities as your teacher assigns.

1. Classify all of the Blue Ribbon words into three separate categories, based on their phonetic respellings or their meanings. You may select *any three categories,* but every word on the list must fit into one of them.

2. Use at least 20 of the Blue Ribbon words in a short story of no longer than 300 words. You may use up to five Blue Ribbon words in the title.

3. Use a word search grid to create your own word search puzzle. Your puzzle should contain at least 15 Blue Ribbon words.

4. Arrange the Blue Ribbon words in "backwards" alphabetical order. In other words, first look at the *last* letter of each word to determine alphabetical order, then at the next-to-last letter, and so forth.

5. From the Blue Ribbon word lists, select the five easiest and the five hardest words to spell. Arrange the five hardest words from most to least difficult. Arrange the five simplest words from easier to easiest. Write a sentence describing why your hardest word was difficult to spell and why your easiest word was a snap.

6. Find as many smaller words as you can in each Blue Ribbon word. You may *not* mix up the letters in the word. For example, the word *example* contains four smaller words: *exam, ample, am,* and *amp.*

7. Write one synonym and one antonym for 15 Blue Ribbon words. Make a chart like this to show your work:

Blue Ribbon word	Synonym	Antonym

8. Write a poem using at least ten Blue Ribbon words. You may want to experiment with a particular poetry form, such as haiku or a cinquain.

9. Change ten Blue Ribbon words into new words by changing no more than three letters in each word. For example, the word *elated* can be changed to the word *flared* by changing the first **e** to **f** and the **t** to **r**. Making nouns plural, changing verb endings, or changing the total number of letters in a word is strictly prohibited.

10. Some of the Blue Ribbon words have several meanings. Research the words in the list and write down a new, unusual, or obscure meaning for at least ten of them. Use each word in a complete sentence that illustrates the unusual meaning you found.

Water, Water, Everywhere

General principle   Some words end with consonant blends such as **ft, lt,** and **nt.**
Read the paragraph below. Your Blue Ribbon words are underlined.

One hot summer's day, the police <u>lieutenant</u> opened the fire
hydrant for Lupe and her friends to cool off in. "I'll be back in an
hour," he told the girls. As the water flowed out, the <u>sediment</u> in
the gutter was washed down the drain. Suddenly Lupe noticed
an <u>iridescent</u> flash in the water. She knelt to take a closer look
at the shiny object in the <u>silt</u>. Lupe picked it up, carefully rinsed
it off, and placed it on the <u>asphalt</u>. Before her gleamed a cobalt
blue sapphire.

1. Write your Blue Ribbon words on a
   sheet of paper.
2. Using a dictionary, write each word's
   phonetic spelling and definition. Then
   write each word in a new sentence.
3. Learn the spelling and definition of
   each Blue Ribbon word. Be prepared
   to write each word, properly spelled,
   in a complete sentence.

2
What will Lupe (in the paragraph above) do with the valuable
jewel she has found? Write a paragraph describing Lupe's
actions. Use as many Blue Ribbon words as possible.
Remember, spelling counts!

3

Lupe's school offered a special summer program to help gifted writers develop their talents. Lupe was chosen for the program. The first thing she wrote was about a young girl and her dog in time of peril.

Read the portion of her story below, filling in each blank with the letters **ft, lt,** or **nt.** Then make a list of the filled-in words. (You should have 15.)

The torre____ of water pushed the fragile life ra____ into the swi____ curre____. Looking behind her, Carmen saw that the a____ section of the ship was still visible, ti____ed upward above the angry sea. Looking back was too difficu____. She turned away and gathered her puppy Somersau____ into the remna____ of a qui____ that she had. Only a so____ tu____ of fur could be seen as the puppy shi____ed his body closer for warmth. They were adri____ on the vast, vaca____ ocean.

4

One rainy afternoon, Lupe and her friends decided to play Hinky Pinky, using only words ending in **ft, lt,** and **nt.** Kevin called out, "I have an **nt** Hink Pink. It's an old man leaning over."

"That's easy," said Angela. "It's a *bent gent.*"

Join the game by filling in the blanks in the answers below. Then design three Hink Pinks of your own, using any rhyming words that end in **ft, lt,** or **nt.**

Clues	Hink Pink
1. an insect's song	an ant _____
2. it made a penny purchase	a spent _____
3. weak coloring pigment for wall	faint _____
4. an easy-going, huge fairy-tale being	a pliant _____
5. an amiable game bird	a pleasant _____
6. _____	_____
7. _____	_____
8. _____	_____

A Matter of Taste

1

General principle   The sound /k/ is usually spelled **c, k,** or **ck.** The **ck** spelling sometimes *ends* a word or syllable, but never starts a word or syllable.

Read the sentences below. Your Blue Ribbon words are underlined.

- Watching my brother try to eat spinach is a <u>comical</u> experience.
- I am <u>contemplating</u> trying chocolate-covered ants at that new gourmet restaurant.
- <u>Broccoli</u> with cheese sauce is not my cup of tea.
- I can't taste any difference between a <u>currant</u> and a raisin.
- You have to be something of a <u>maverick</u> to feed your dog barbecued steak every night.

1. Write your Blue Ribbon words on a sheet of paper.
2. Using a dictionary, write each word's phonetic spelling and definition. Then write each word in a new sentence.
3. Learn the spelling and definition of each Blue Ribbon word. Be prepared to write each word, properly spelled, in a complete sentence.

2

The adjectives listed below can be used to describe the taste and texture of food. Use each word to describe a food you have eaten. Circle each word in which the letter **c** stands for the /k/ sound.

1. acrid _____
2. delectable _____
3. luscious _____
4. spicy _____
5. scrumptious _____
6. curdled _____
7. condensed _____
8. congealed _____
9. chewy _____
10. crumbly _____
11. crisp _____
12. scalding-hot _____
13. crunchy _____
14. sticky _____
15. viscous _____
16. coarse _____
17. creamy _____
18. thickened _____
19. scrambled _____
20. saccharine _____

3

The house specialty at the Come On Inn restaurant is a delicious vegetable chowder. One day when the head chef became ill, her assistant had to make the chowder. Unfortunately, the ingredients in the chef's recipe were scribbled on a piece of paper along with some cooking utensils she intended to purchase.

Organize the 20 items into two separate lists, food and cooking utensils, for the panic-stricken assistant.

sieve	artichoke	spatula	corer
maize	kohlrabi	leek	ricer
colander	chard	scallion	pestle
kale	coriander	lentil	whisk
okra	casserole	crock	cleaver

4

To solve this problem, you need to use deductive reasoning. The chart will help you.

Read the clues. Whenever you learn what someone did NOT eat, write an 0 in that box on the chart. When three boxes in any row or column are filled with 0's, write an X in the box that's left. The X's tell you the solution.

Problem Mom, Gramps, Laura, and Patrick went to a restaurant. The new waiter took their orders and returned with a broiled hamburger, an egg-salad grinder, a tossed salad with onions, and a fried fish sandwich. Unfortunately, he could not remember who ordered what. He had, however, overheard the family discussing their likes and dislikes.

Use the clues from their conversation to solve the problem. The clues about Laura are already recorded for you.

Clues
1. Laura hates fish and broiled foods.
2. Mom doesn't like onions or fried foods.
3. Gramps is a vegetarian and doesn't eat meat or fish.
4. Patrick never eats eggs or hamburger.
5. Gramps is allergic to eggs.

	salad	fried fish	egg grinder	hamburger
Laura		O		O
Mom				
Gramps				
Patrick				

Believe It or Not

1

General principle   The vowel sound /ou/ heard in words like *owl* and *trout* is usually spelled **ow** or **ou.**

Read the paragraph below. Your Blue Ribbon words are underlined.

     Superguy is <u>endowed</u> with the ability to leap tall buildings. Criminals crouch in corners to avoid a <u>trouncing</u> from Superguy. He has only one flaw: a <u>towering</u> fondness for sweets. One day a crowd was <u>astounded</u> to see Superguy beg for a little girl's lollipop. He stuck it in his mouth, then disappeared into the air with a single bound, flying off once again to <u>oust</u> criminals from their hideouts.

1. Write your Blue Ribbon words on a sheet of paper.
2. Using a dictionary, write each word's phonetic spelling and definition. Then write each word in a new sentence.
3. Learn the spelling and definition of each Blue Ribbon word. Be prepared to write each word, properly spelled, in a complete sentence.

2

This coded message was left for Superguy by reporter Stacey Street. In order to confound the thieves who had stolen a precious item from a museum, she left blanks for all /ow/ sounds in the words. Decode the message.

> I f___nd the cr___wn on the gr___nd near the fl___er
>
> garden behind the h___se. The crooks are pr___ling ab___t
>
> the t___n. P___nce on them and imp___nd them n___!

3

"As fast as a speeding rocket" is a comparison, or figure of speech, that describes Superguy. It is called a *simile.* Usually the word *as* or *like* is used in a simile, comparing two unlike things.

The similes below are as "old as the hills," and that makes them *clichés.* Substitute a new idea for each word in parentheses in the clichés below. Your new similes should be "fresh as a daisy."

1. quick as (a wink) _____

2. white as (a sheet) _____

3. light as (a feather) _____

4. mad as (a hornet) _____

5. easy as (pie) _____

6. slow as (molasses) _____

7. straight as (an arrow) _____

8. sharp as (a tack) _____

9. neat as (a pin) _____

10. hard as (a rock) _____

4

Having x-ray vision allows Superguy to spot anything amiss in a scene or group of objects. Can you spot the "stranger" in each group of words below?

Circle the word that does not belong with the others. Explain the reason for your choice. You may have to use your dictionary.

Example   fowl   flower   frown   (flown)
Flown does not belong because *ow* is pronounced /ō/ in this word.

1. growl   show   shower   fowl

_____

2. renown   scow   glower   aglow

_____

3. slouch   impound   though   scour

_____

4. profound   trounce   uncouth   surmount

_____

Out of This World

1

General principle   The /ėr/ sound of a vowel with **r** can have several different spellings.

Read the sentences below. Your Blue Ribbon words are underlined.

- Officials <u>confirmed</u> that a satellite was launched yesterday from Cape Canaveral.
- The spaceship <u>terminal</u> was off-limits during the launch.
- Scientists <u>authorized</u> Mission Control to jettison the booster.
- The spacecraft <u>hurtled</u> through space towards Pluto.
- Instruments on board sent back new scientific information about the <u>solar</u> system.

1. Write your Blue Ribbon words on a sheet of paper.

2. Using a dictionary, write each word's phonetic spelling and definition. Then write each word in a new sentence.

3. Learn the spelling and definition of each Blue Ribbon word. Be prepared to write each word, properly spelled, in a complete sentence.

2

The message below is relayed to Earth from a malfunctioning computer on a flight of the Surveyor probe to the planet Pluto. The on-flight computer is not printing any word that contains the sound /ėr/.

Translate and recopy the message, adding all the missing letters. Remember: When you encounter a set of blanks, say /ėr/ and then spell the word correctly.

Our instruments show a sol___ dist___bance. The ship

crossed through a meteor show___. Yest___day S___vey___

was damaged in a crat___ on the lun___ s___face. We are

experiencing t___bulence now. We are approaching the

out___ bound___y of Jupit___. Ov___ and out.

3

You don't need to travel out of this world to encounter strange beings, as the answers to these questions will demonstrate. What creature in the world has the sound /ėr/ in its name and . . .

1. has a long sticky tongue for eating insects? _____

2. has an exoskeleton? _____

3. lives in tide pools and resembles a plant? _____

4. eats houses? _____

5. is a huge pachyderm with a vertical horn on its snout? _____

6. would make the first string basketball team? _____

7. is a reptile with appendages? _____

4

As the satellite circles the unexplored planet, it radios back to earth a description of the features it detects. Circle as many as you can find in the puzzle, then write them in a list. The 12 hidden words read either straight across or straight down.

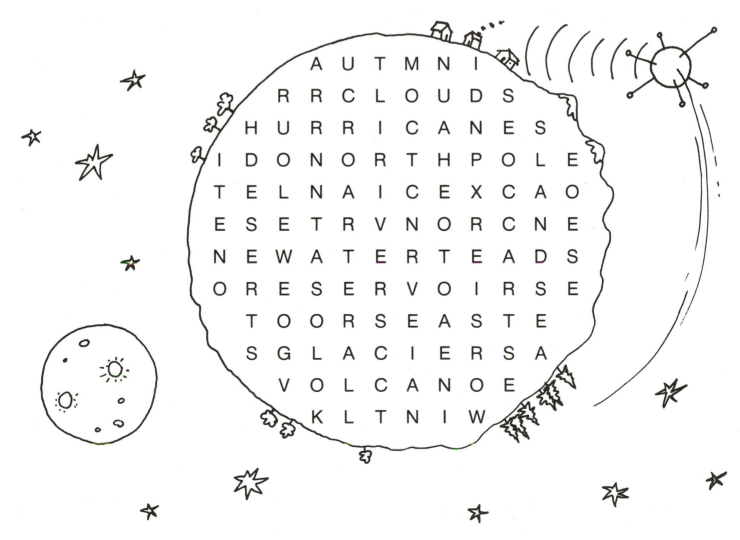

vowels with r

Little White Lies

1

General principle   Some vowel spellings do not follow any rules. You must memorize the spelling of some words that contain **au** or **aw.**

Read the sentences below. Your Blue Ribbon words are underlined.

- Said the princess to the thief: "This jewel is just a <u>gaudy</u> bauble."
- Said the used car dealer to the blind man: "The paint job on this car is <u>flawless</u>."
- Said the door-to-door salesman to the customer: "What do you take me for, a <u>fraud</u>?"
- Said the fisherwoman to her friend: "I know this doesn't sound <u>plausible</u>, but the fish that got away was four feet long!"
- Said the autograph dealer: "This worthless looking <u>scrawl</u> is George Washington's signature!"

1. Write your Blue Ribbon words on a sheet of paper.
2. Using a dictionary, write each word's phonetic spelling and definition. Then write each word in a new sentence.
3. Learn the spelling and definition of each Blue Ribbon word. Be prepared to write each word, properly spelled, in a complete sentence.

2

These words are synonyms for the words *truthful* and *deceitful.* Use a dictionary to help you define each word.

1. genuine _____
2. authentic _____
3. candid _____
4. veracious _____
5. mendacious _____
6. forthright _____
7. false _____
8. gospel _____
9. shifty _____
10. wily _____

3

Would you believe that some of these word pairs rhyme and others do not, yet each pair has the same final letters? Mark T (for true) by the words that rhyme, and F (for false) by those that do *not* rhyme. Use a dictionary if necessary to check pronunciations.

1. sleight and freight _____

2. break and bleak _____

3. mallet and ballet _____

4. grown and frown _____

5. chow and show _____

6. terse and verse _____

7. pool and wool _____

8. hoot and soot _____

9. tribe and bribe _____

10. bower and mower _____

4

1. The following two quotes say the same thing in different ways. Write a sentence that summarizes the meaning of the quotes. Remember, spelling counts!

   "The telling of a falsehood is like the cut of a sabre; for though the wound may heal, the scar will remain."
   —Saadi

   "A lie, though it be killed and dead, can sting sometimes like a dead wasp."
   —Anna Jameson

   _____

   _____

   _____

2. These next two quotes express a different opinion about lying. Write a sentence that summarizes the meaning of these two quotes.

   "Never chase a lie. Let it alone, deny it water and sunlight, and it will wither away and die."
   —Lyman Beecher

   "A lie is like a great fish on dry land. It may fret and fling and make a frightful bother, but it cannot hurt you. You have only to keep still and it will die of itself."
   —George Crabbe

   _____

   _____

   _____

Blue Ribbon Review Lesson

Your Blue Ribbon Review Words

lieutenant, sediment, iridescent, silt, asphalt

comical, contemplating, broccoli, currant, maverick

endowed, trouncing, towering, astounded, oust

confirmed, terminal, authorized, hurtled, solar

gaudy, flawless, fraud, plausible, scrawl

Review Activities

Use your Blue Ribbon review words to complete as many of the following activities as your teacher assigns.

1. Classify all of the Blue Ribbon words into three separate categories, based on their phonetic respellings or their meanings. You may select *any three categories,* but every word on the list must fit into one of them.

2. Use at least 20 of the Blue Ribbon words in a short story of no longer than 300 words. You may use up to five Blue Ribbon words in the title.

3. Use a word search grid to create your own word search puzzle. Your puzzle should contain at least 15 Blue Ribbon words.

4. Arrange the Blue Ribbon words in "backwards" alphabetical order. In other words, first look at the *last* letter of each word to determine alphabetical order, then at the next-to-last letter, and so forth.

5. From the Blue Ribbon word lists, select the five easiest and the five hardest words to spell. Arrange the five hardest words from most to least difficult. Arrange the five simplest words from easier to easiest. Write a sentence describing why your hardest word was difficult to spell and why your easiest word was a snap.

6. Find as many smaller words as you can in each Blue Ribbon word. You may *not* mix up the letters in the word. For example, the word *example* contains four smaller words: *exam, ample, am,* and *amp.*

7. Write one synonym and one antonym for 15 Blue Ribbon words. Make a chart like this to show your work:

Blue Ribbon word	Synonym	Antonym

8. Write a poem using at least ten Blue Ribbon words. You may want to experiment with a particular poetry form, such as haiku or a cinquain.

9. Change ten Blue Ribbon words into new words by changing no more than three letters in each word. For example, the word *elated* can be changed to the word *flared* by changing the first **e** to **f** and the **t** to **r.** Making nouns plural, changing verb endings, or changing the total number of letters in a word is strictly prohibited.

10. Some of the Blue Ribbon words have several meanings. Research the words in the list and write down a new, unusual, or obscure meaning for at least ten of them. Use each word in a complete sentence that illustrates the unusual meaning you found.

Don't Bug Me

1   General principle

Compound words are two words used together as one word. Some compound words, *closed* compounds, are written as a single word. *Open* compounds are written with a space between words, and other compounds have a hyphen between words.

Read the sentences below. Your Blue Ribbon words are underlined.

- The <u>swallowtail</u> butterfly is protected from insect-eating birds because it is highly unpalatable.
- The <u>dragonfly</u> is also known as the devil's darning needle, following the superstition that it may sew up the eyes, ears, and mouth of a sleeping child.
- <u>Silverfish</u> are not fish at all, but live indoors and feed on materials that contain large amounts of starch, such as books and flour.
- Since the <u>praying mantis</u> devours other insects alive, some people call it a "preying mantis."
- The <u>cockroach</u>, one of the oldest fossil insects, is mashed with sugar by some tribal medicine men and applied to sores to promote healing.

1. Write your Blue Ribbon words on a sheet of paper.
2. Using a dictionary, write each word's phonetic spelling and definition. Then write each word in a new sentence.
3. Learn the spelling and definition of each Blue Ribbon word. Be prepared to write each word, properly spelled, in a complete sentence.

2

Compound words are often used for the names of common insects and spiders. List at least 20 open and closed compound words naming insects or spiders.

_____   _____   _____   _____

_____   _____   _____   _____

_____   _____   _____   _____

_____   _____   _____   _____

_____   _____   _____   _____

3

Nominate ten insects in these categories for the "Book of World-Record Bugs."

1. World's biggest nuisance _____

2. World's most minute _____

3. World's most vociferous _____

4. World's most gargantuan _____

5. World's most destructive _____

6. World's most odiferous _____

7. World's most appendages _____

8. World's most numerous _____

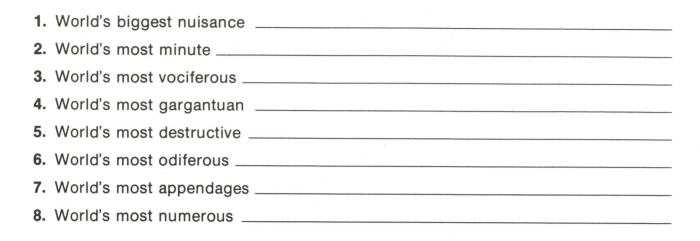

4

People often say "That bugs me" when something annoying is happening. This word search contains 24 synonyms for the slang word "bug." Circle as many as you can find, then write them in a list. The hidden words read either straight across or straight down.

```
A A M A D D E N H S T O M E R S
B N I N F U R I A T E L E A A F
R N R P E R T U R B A L O X N R
A O R U F F L E A R S A N P G U
D Y I R K O N E S H E C K L E S
E F T U P S E T S S H E A A R T
C H A F E A R O L E N R A G E R
I N T E S I N C E N S E N U O A
B V E X T A G G R A V A T E A T
L E A D E X A S P E R A T E E E
E X C P R O V O K E B O T H E R
```

compound words

Happy Holidays

1

General principle Holiday names and the word *day* as part of a holiday name begin with capital letters.

Read the sentences below. Your Blue Ribbon words are underlined.

- Memorial Day used to be called Decoration Day because people decorated graves with flowers.
- Almost every state has its own Admission Day, but that doesn't mean they charge admission to get in.
- Independence Day falls in July in the United States, but in September in Mexico.
- Mardi Gras is celebrated each year in Louisiana.
- Alaska is the only state that doesn't observe Arbor Day.

1. Write your Blue Ribbon words on a sheet of paper.
2. Using a dictionary, write each word's phonetic spelling and definition. Then write each word in a new sentence.
3. Learn the spelling and definition of each Blue Ribbon word. Be prepared to write each word, properly spelled, in a complete sentence.

2

Holidays that celebrate the birth of an important person are usually declared posthumously (after a person has died). Nominate three living persons whose birthdays, in your opinion, should be considered for selection as national holidays. State your reasons for each choice. Remember, spelling counts!

1. _____
   _____
   _____

2. _____
   _____
   _____

3. _____
   _____
   _____

3

Each of these objects is associated with one or more holidays. Write a sentence describing how each one is used for a particular holiday.

1. pyrotechnics _____

2. cornucopia _____

3. menorah _____

4. nosegay _____

5. confetti _____

6. crèche _____

7. masquerades _____

8. piñata _____

9. ballot _____

10. specter _____

4

Many stores and businesses depend either partially or wholly on holidays, celebrations, and vacations for their livelihood. List at least ten of these. Remember, spelling counts!

1. _____

2. _____

3. _____

4. _____

5. _____

6. _____

7. _____

8. _____

9. _____

10. _____

Mind Your Manners

1

General principle   The prefixes **in-**, **im-**, **un-**, and **ir-** usually make words mean the opposite of what they meant before. These prefixes are *negative* prefixes.

Read the paragraphs below. Your Blue Ribbon words are underlined.

The entire lunchroom was about to be punished for the <u>imprudent</u> behavior of a few fourth graders.

"I am not being <u>unreasonable</u>," the principal declared as he surveyed the carrots and peas strewn under the tables. "This mess is clearly the result of <u>immaturity</u>. If those <u>irresponsible</u> students who caused the disaster will step forward and clean it up, I will be lenient."

"I suppose we really were <u>inconsiderate</u>," a small group of girls admitted.

1. Write your Blue Ribbon words on a sheet of paper.
2. Using a dictionary, write each word's phonetic spelling and definition. Then write each word in a new sentence.
3. Learn the spelling and definition of each Blue Ribbon word. Be prepared to write each word, properly spelled, in a complete sentence.

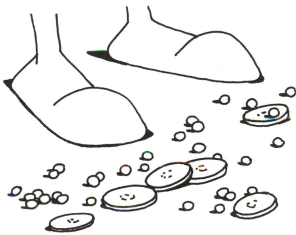

2

For each word below, find a synonym with a negative prefix and write it in the blank beside the word.

1. boastful _____
2. insensitive _____
3. intact _____
4. mysterious _____
5. weak _____
6. memorable _____
7. peerless _____
8. rude _____
9. tainted _____

Synonyms
unforgettable
immodest
infirm
impolite
uncanny
undamaged
unequaled
unfeeling
impure

3

Adults constantly remind children to follow rules and to "mind their manners." Sometimes children think that adults begin every sentence with the word "DON'T. . . ."

"Don't interrupt." "Don't talk with your mouth full of food." "Don't talk back." These are just a few examples. If children could make rules for adults to follow, what would they recommend?

Write five rules of your own for adults. Each rule must contain a word with the negative prefix **in-**, **im-**, or **un-**.

Example Adults should not give children *indigestion* at dinner by yelling at them to chew with their mouths closed.

1. _____

   _____

2. _____

   _____

3. _____

   _____

4. _____

   _____

5. _____

   _____

4

An *analogy* is a special type of comparison between two things or ideas. *"Key* is to *unlock* as *corkscrew* is to *uncork"* is an analogy.

Fill in the blanks in each of these comparisons to make an accurate analogy.

1. *Shoe* is to *unlace* as _____ is to *unbutton.*

2. A *writer* is to a *book* as _____ is to a *picture.*

3. A *napkin* is to a *lap* as _____ is to a *table.*

4. A *clock* is to *time* as _____ is to *temperature.*

Now write two analogies of your own.

5. _____ is to _____ as

   _____ is to _____ .

6. _____ is to _____ as

   _____ is to _____ .

What's So Funny?

1 _____

General principle   The consonant sound /j/ is usually spelled **j** or **g**.

Read the paragraphs below. Your Blue Ribbon words are underlined.

  Mr. Guffaw is a <u>jovial</u> person most of the time. He insists that our entire class is <u>obliged</u> to laugh at his jokes. Unfortunately, the <u>majority</u> of us have heard his jokes at least ten times each.
  "Can't you <u>indulge</u> your poor old teacher and laugh anyway?" he pleads.
  "Can't you <u>generate</u> some new jokes?" we always reply in jest.

1. Write your Blue Ribbon words on a sheet of paper.
2. Using a dictionary, write each word's phonetic spelling and definition. Then write each word in a new sentence.
3. Learn the spelling and definition of each Blue Ribbon word. Be prepared to write each word, properly spelled, in a complete sentence.

2 _____

Mr. Guffaw likes *malapropisms.* These are blunders that people make when they use a word that *sounds like* what they mean, but isn't. It always sounds funny if you know the difference. The term is named after a fictional character, Mrs. Malaprop, who constantly made this kind of error.

Rewrite at least one word in each sentence below to fix the malapropism.

1. He was so hungry, he gouged himself.

2. The best way to eat cream cheese and lox is with a beagle.

3. A doctor uses epidemic needles to give shots.

4. Our class had a car wash as a fun raiser for the field trip.

5. The baseball player said, "I saw the Umpire State Building in New York."

6. A camellia changes the color of its skin to hide from danger.

j and soft g   **43**

3

One day during a lesson on adverbs, Mr. Guffaw wrote the following example on the board:

"I wasn't there for the test," the student said *absently.*

A sentence that makes a joke with the adverb this way is called a "Tom Swifty." That's another one of Mr. Guffaw's specialties.

Here's Mr. Guffaw's homework assignment: "Use each of the following adverbs in a complete sentence. Try to emulate my wit and style by writing Tom Swifties—if you can."

1. energetically _____

_____

2. gingerly _____

_____

3. rigidly _____

_____

4. intelligently _____

_____

5. engagingly _____

_____

4

"Spoonerisms" are another favorite of Mr. Guffaw's. The term comes from a British minister, Mr. Spooner, who had a noticeable problem delivering his sermons: he would switch the initial sounds in words. "Sporks and foons," for example, is a spoonerism for "forks and spoons."

Use five of the spoonerisms listed below, plus some of your own, in a humorous paragraph.

kugs and hisses   gop and sto   mat and couse
nins and peedles   rops and cobbers   tow and shell
shight and briny   fost and lound   palt and sepper

Going, Going, Gone

1

General principle   Most plural nouns are formed by adding **-s** to the singular form. We add **-es** to words ending in **x, ch, sh, s, ss,** and sometimes **o.**

Read the sentences below. Your Blue Ribbon words are underlined.

- <u>Platypuses</u>, protected by law in Australia, often resemble pieces of floating debris when they swim.
- Chambered <u>nautiluses</u>, members of an order that has lived on earth for millions of years, help scientists determine the date of strata in which their fossils are found.
- The Arabian oryx is becoming extinct because hunting parties use cars and planes to overtake <u>oryxes</u> as they graze.
- The <u>carcasses</u> of Ceylon elephants, an endangered species, are mute evidence of the anger of the farmers whose fields they destroy.
- Several endangered species of birds find refuge in the <u>bulrushes</u> that grow along rivers and streams.

1. Write your Blue Ribbon words on a sheet of paper.
2. Using a dictionary, write each word's phonetic spelling and definition. Then write each word in a new sentence.
3. Learn the spelling and definition of each Blue Ribbon word. Be prepared to write each word, properly spelled, in a complete sentence.

2

Groups of animals often have special collective names. These words are used with the plurals of the animal names. A group of fish, for example, is called a *school* of fish.

Match each of these animals with its group name. Use your dictionary if necessary.

pack	litter	troop
herd	skulk	gaggle
swarm	sloth	colony
pride	clowder	pod
flock	rafter	bevy

1. a _____ of bears
2. a _____ of cats
3. a _____ of foxes
4. a _____ of horses
5. a _____ of turkeys

6. a _____ of beavers
7. a _____ of chickens
8. a _____ of geese
9. a _____ of pigs
10. a _____ of monkeys
11. a _____ of bees
12. a _____ of dogs
13. a _____ of lions
14. a _____ of seals
15. a _____ of quails

3

Things besides animals can become endangered or extinct. Horse-drawn carriages and Model-T Fords are forms of transportation that are only seen as antiques these days. Certain inventions such as a butter churn became extinct when dairies began to use electricity to turn cream into butter. Even words can become extinct. Whoever says "bumbershoot" anymore for an umbrella?

Identify each of the ten extinct items below. Then name four of your own to stump your teacher and classmates.

1. knickers _____
2. flappers _____
3. bustles _____
4. buttonhooks _____
5. pommades _____
6. styluses _____
7. monocles _____
8. beatniks _____
9. parasols _____
10. victrolas _____
11. _____
12. _____
13. _____
14. _____

4

Many human beings talk about—and some believe in—animals that have never been proven to exist. Choose one of the five creatures below and write a paragraph describing some of the beliefs that people have about it. Underline every plural noun you use.

a centaur
the Loch Ness monster
Big Foot
a phoenix
a unicorn

Blue Ribbon Review Lesson

Your Blue Ribbon Review Words

swallowtail, dragonfly, silverfish, praying mantis, cockroach

Memorial Day, Admission Day, Independence Day, Mardi Gras,
  Arbor Day

imprudent, unreasonable, immaturity, irresponsible, inconsiderate

jovial, obliged, majority, indulge, generate

platypuses, nautiluses, oryxes, carcasses, bulrushes

Review Activities

Use your Blue Ribbon review words to complete as many of the
following activities as your teacher assigns.

1. Classify all of the Blue Ribbon words into three separate
   categories, based on their phonetic respellings or their
   meanings. You may select *any three categories,* but every
   word on the list must fit into one of them.

2. Use at least 20 of the Blue Ribbon words in a short story of
   no longer than 300 words. You may use up to five Blue
   Ribbon words in the title.

3. Use a word search grid to create your own word search
   puzzle. Your puzzle should contain at least 15 Blue Ribbon
   words.

4. Arrange the Blue Ribbon words in "backwards" alphabetical
   order. In other words, first look at the *last* letter of each
   word to determine alphabetical order, then at the next-to-
   last letter, and so forth.

5. From the Blue Ribbon word lists, select the five easiest and
   the five hardest words to spell. Arrange the five hardest
   words from most to least difficult. Arrange the five simplest
   words from easier to easiest. Write a sentence describing
   why your hardest word was difficult to spell and why your
   easiest word was a snap.

6. Find as many smaller words as you can in each Blue Ribbon word. You may *not* mix up the letters in the word. For example, the word *example* contains four smaller words: *exam, ample, am,* and *amp.*

7. Write one synonym and one antonym for 15 Blue Ribbon words. Make a chart like this to show your work:

Blue Ribbon word	Synonym	Antonym

8. Write a poem using at least ten Blue Ribbon words. You may want to experiment with a particular poetry form, such as haiku or a cinquain.

9. Change ten Blue Ribbon words into new words by changing no more than three letters in each word. For example, the word *elated* can be changed to the word *flared* by changing the first **e** to **f** and the **t** to **r.** Making nouns plural, changing verb endings, or changing the total number of letters in a word is strictly prohibited.

10. Some of the Blue Ribbon words have several meanings. Research the words in the list and write down a new, unusual, or obscure meaning for at least ten of them. Use each word in a complete sentence that illustrates the unusual meaning you found.

Just Desserts

1

General principle   Two common ways to spell /s/ are **s** and **c**.

Read the sentences below. Your Blue Ribbon words are underlined.

- Lucille wasn't hungry when served liver and onions for dinner, but she was <u>ravenous</u> when she saw the chocolate cake for dessert.
- Mincemeat pie was Lance's favorite dessert until he learned that it contained <u>suet</u>.
- Who ever heard of a sundae with <u>cinnamon</u> syrup?
- Sarah's grandmother makes the best <u>crescent</u> shaped butter cookies.
- That hot fudge sundae looks <u>luscious</u>!

1. Write your Blue Ribbon words on a sheet of paper.
2. Using a dictionary, write each word's phonetic spelling and definition. Then write each word in a new sentence.
3. Learn the spelling and definition of each Blue Ribbon word. Be prepared to write each word, properly spelled, in a complete sentence.

2

One famous ice cream store advertises 31 flavors to attract customers. List as many flavors as you can that might be on an ice cream menu. Place a star next to any flavor name that contains the sound /s/—you'll get an extra scoop for these.

_____   _____   _____   _____

_____   _____   _____   _____

_____   _____   _____   _____

_____   _____   _____   _____

_____   _____   _____   _____

_____   _____   _____   _____

_____   _____   _____   _____

3

Write a description of your favorite dessert in 50 words or more. Describe your special treat so that your friends will be clamoring to taste it. Hint: Use adjectives that appeal to the senses. Include a tantalizing picture, too.

4

Cynthia's mother went on a business trip one day. When Cynthia returned home from school, she found this note. Complete the note by filling in each blank with a word that contains the /s/ sound. You must use *all* the words on the list.

floss
exceptionally
piece
dessert
consume
cider
morsel
slice
delicious
insist
absolutely
soda
disregarding
suspension
supper
serious
casserole

Dearest Family:

   I am leaving an _____ _____ chocolate cake on the counter for your _____. Do not _____ this cake before _____. I _____ that you finish every _____ of _____ before you _____ a _____. You may have milk or _____ with the cake—_____ no _____ tonight! _____ my orders will result in a _____ of privileges. I am _____!

                                        Your loving mother

P.S. Brush and _____
    your teeth before bed!

Double Play

1 **General principle** For one-syllable verbs like *tap* that end with a single vowel followed by a single consonant, double the final consonant when adding **-ed**, **-ing**, or **-er**.

Read the paragraphs below. Your Blue Ribbon words are underlined.

The baseball stands were <u>crammed</u> with friends and relatives for the home team's championship game. The local baseball team, the West Kingston Twins, <u>donned</u> their gloves and raced ecstatically onto the field after the tying runner scored. The pitcher, an eleven-year-old <u>dubbed</u> "Flash," took the mound and confidently pitched to the batter, who hit the ball and threw the bat deliberately at the first baseman.

The umpire ran to home plate and bellowed at the batter, "I'm <u>banning</u> you from the game for intentionally throwing the bat!" The evicted runner <u>trekked</u> dejectedly back to the bench.

1. Write your Blue Ribbon words on a sheet of paper.
2. Using a dictionary, write each word's phonetic spelling and definition. Then write each word in a new sentence.
3. Learn the spelling and definition of each Blue Ribbon word. Be prepared to write each word, properly spelled, in a complete sentence.

2 The coach made the following speech to her team after the game. Locate and copy below ten words in her game summary that are in some way related to the concept "double." Then write three words from the speech that are spelled with double consonants, *according to the general principle above.*

"That was a stunning twofold victory for the West Kingston Twins. Even though we were paired with an unbeaten team, we took the double-header and won the championship. In the first half of the second inning I thought the umpire needed bifocals when he called our runners out at the plate twice. I held my breath when the outfield missed a couple of pop flys. The score tells the story, however. I hope we can duplicate our winning season next year."

"Double" words

1. _____
2. _____
3. _____
4. _____
5. _____
6. _____
7. _____
8. _____
9. _____
10. _____

Double-consonant words

1. _____
2. _____
3. _____

Double Play—page 2

3

_____

Some words are associated in pairs by meaning. "Cup and saucer" is one example of such word twins. Name three more sets of word twins. Then use any three of the following word twins in sentences.

footloose and fancy free   hill and dale   _____

hither and yon   cease and desist   _____

cut and dried   ebb and flow   _____

1. _____

2. _____

3. _____

4

_____

This baseball-diamond word search contains 17 one-syllable words in which you double the final consonant before adding -ed or -ing. Each word is in the shape of a diamond, and must be spelled "in order" around the bases, starting at the top.

```
              C  T
            H  R  P  P
         D  C  O  I  P  F
       R  L  G  P  L  R  T  T
     D  D  A  A  S  S  O  E  S  P
   E  R  F  P  P  L  R  M  P  L  T  N
     L  I  P  S  U  A  R  S  O  A
       A  N  T  P  S  K  N  D
         R  I  P  S  N  I
            A  L  A  P
              G  I
```

Example   FLAP

Hint: Each word begins with a consonant blend.

Write the past tense of each word you find hidden in the puzzle.

1. _flapped_   **7.** _____   **13.** _____

2. _____   **8.** _____   **14.** _____

3. _____   **9.** _____   **15.** _____

4. _____   **10.** _____   **16.** _____

5. _____   **11.** _____   **17.** _____

6. _____   **12.** _____

Little by Little

1

General principle When verbs end in the letter **e,** we usually drop the **e** before adding **-ed** or **-ing.** For example: *stare + ing = staring.*

Read the paragraph below. Your Blue Ribbon words are underlined.

    The world's supply of natural renewable resources is <u>dwindling</u>. Each year the reserves are <u>decreasing</u> as people continue to act as if the supply is endless. Conservationists, the people who work to preserve energy, are often <u>belittled</u> for their efforts. <u>Reducing</u> consumption and developing new methods for producing energy are two of their solutions to the problem. Fortunately, the heavy use of natural gas <u>abated</u> last year because of the mild winter.

1. Write your Blue Ribbon words on a sheet of paper.
2. Using a dictionary, write each word's phonetic spelling and definition. Then write each word in a new sentence.
3. Learn the spelling and definition of each Blue Ribbon word. Be prepared to write each word, properly spelled, in a complete sentence.

2

The five adjectives below *describe* little things, and the five nouns *name* little things. Write a sentence using each word.

Adjectives
petite
miniscule
diminutive
miniature
microscopic

Nouns
mite
speck
smidgen
midget
molecule

3

Each of the common expressions below centers around the concept of *little vs. big.* Describe in your own words what each expression means, and give an example that proves the point.

1. Big things come in little packages.

_____

_____

_____

2. Great oaks from little acorns grow.

_____

_____

_____

_____

_____

3. A little goes a long way.

_____

_____

_____

4. It's the little things in life that count.

_____

_____

_____

4

The word *lilliputian* means "tiny" or "of little size." Write at least 30 smaller words using the letters in that word.

You may not use any letter more than once in a word, except for **L** or **I,** which you may use three times each (as in *lilliputian).*

LILLIPUTIAN

1. _____	7. _____	13. _____	19. _____	25. _____
2. _____	8. _____	14. _____	20. _____	26. _____
3. _____	9. _____	15. _____	21. _____	27. _____
4. _____	10. _____	16. _____	22. _____	28. _____
5. _____	11. _____	17. _____	23. _____	29. _____
6. _____	12. _____	18. _____	24. _____	30. _____

Better Sopper-Uppers

1 **General principle**   Drop the final **e** or change the final **y** to **i** before you add **-er** or **-est** to make comparative words.

Read the paragraph below. Your Blue Ribbon words are underlined.

Sopperup paper towels are the <u>heftiest</u> in the business. Other paper towels get <u>soggier</u> more quickly. Sopperups absorb <u>grimier</u>, sloppier messes more speedily. In fact, Sopperups are just plain <u>ornerier</u> about messes than any other paper towel. The fact that they are also the <u>thriftiest</u> sopper-upper makes them the best buy on the market for wiping up boo-boos.

1. Write your Blue Ribbon words on a sheet of paper.
2. Using a dictionary, write each word's phonetic spelling and definition. Then write each word in a new sentence.
3. Learn the spelling and definition of each Blue Ribbon word. Be prepared to write each word, properly spelled, in a complete sentence.

2 Each of the items listed below has been used to absorb or eliminate excess water or other fluids from the environment. Explain in a complete sentence what each item accomplishes.

1. caulking _____
2. dehumidifiers _____
3. sandbags _____
4. gauze compresses _____
5. dikes _____
6. cornstarch _____

Name ten other substances that have been used to handle a water or fluid problem.

1. _____   6. _____
2. _____   7. _____
3. _____   8. _____
4. _____   9. _____
5. _____   10. _____

3

Each of the clues below describes a word that ends in *-est.*
None of these words are used, however, to make comparisons.
Read the definition and fill in the blanks.

1. to object   p r __ __ e s t

2. humble   __ __ __ e s t

3. to propose   __ __ __ __ e s t

4. a wish   __ __ __ __ e s t

5. truthful   __ __ __ e s t

6. to joke   __ e s t

7. to reap   __ __ __ __ e s t

8. a competition   __ __ __ __ e s t

9. to hate   __ __ __ e s t

10. to process food
    in the stomach   __ __ __ e s t

4

Some comparisons have been used so often that they lose their
impact on the reader. These comparisons are described as *trite*
or commonplace. The name given to such comparisons is
cliché, which means a trite word or phrase. Rewrite each of the
following clichés to make them less shopworn.

1. cleaner than (a whistle) _____

2. stronger than (an ox) _____

3. skinnier than (a rail) _____

4. smoother than (silk) _____

5. flatter than (a pancake) _____

6. stiffer than (a board) _____

7. happier than (a lark) _____

Same But Different

1

General principle   Homophones are words that sound the same but have different meanings and, often, different spellings.

Read the paragraph below. Your Blue Ribbon words are underlined.

During the American Revolution a small <u>corps</u> of men from Boston, Massachusetts, were ready to fight on a minute's notice. They <u>mustered</u> troops in Massachusetts and other neighboring colonies. These were called "Minutemen," and they became a <u>symbol</u> of America's budding patriotism. The troops were a motley crew compared to the British soldiers, who marched in uniform to a drum <u>roll</u>. Still, the spirits of the colonists <u>soared</u> when they saw the Minutemen coming.

1. Write your Blue Ribbon words on a sheet of paper.
2. Using a dictionary, write each word's phonetic spelling and definition. Then write each word in a new sentence.
3. Learn the spelling and definition of each Blue Ribbon word. Be prepared to write each word, properly spelled, in a complete sentence.

2

Use the *homophone* of each Blue Ribbon word above in a complete sentence.

1. _____

   _____

2. _____

   _____

3. _____

   _____

4. _____

   _____

5. _____

   _____

3

Heteronyms are words that are spelled the same but have completely different meanings. They are also pronounced differently. The word *live,* for example, is pronounced /līv/ as in "a live wire," or /liv/ as in "I live here."

Use each of these heteronyms in two sentences, demonstrating their two different meanings.

1. sow _____

_____

2. tear _____

_____

3. wind _____

_____

4. desert _____

_____

5. record _____

_____

6. close _____

_____

4

This letter was received by the family of a young 16-year-old Minuteman who quit school to join the revolutionary army. Unfortunately, he had missed the lessons on homophones. Proofread and correct his letter, writing the proper form of each word.

My deer family,

I have mist ewe these many daze. As I wrest hear righting to yew, I here the peel of thunder and sea the flair of lightning. The rode is filled with currants of reign water. Hour hoarses sink in the mud and nay in pane. Too buoys dyed yesterday. At thymes I lose hart and I wonder if I am a cowered. I wish this wore wood end.

Yore sun

Sol

Blue Ribbon Review Lesson

Your Blue Ribbon Review Words

ravenous, suet, cinnamon, crescent, luscious

crammed, donned, dubbed, banning, trekked

dwindling, decreasing, belittled, reducing, abated

heftiest, soggier, grimier, ornerier, thriftiest

corps, mustered, symbol, roll, soared

Review Activities

Use your Blue Ribbon review words to complete as many of the following activities as your teacher assigns.

1. Classify all of the Blue Ribbon words into three separate categories, based on their phonetic respellings or their meanings. You may select *any three categories,* but every word on the list must fit into one of them.

2. Use at least 20 of the Blue Ribbon words in a short story of no longer than 300 words. You may use up to five Blue Ribbon words in the title.

3. Use a word search grid to create your own word search puzzle. Your puzzle should contain at least 15 Blue Ribbon words.

4. Arrange the Blue Ribbon words in "backwards" alphabetical order. In other words, first look at the *last* letter of each word to determine alphabetical order, then at the next-to-last letter, and so forth.

5. From the Blue Ribbon word lists, select the five easiest and the five hardest words to spell. Arrange the five hardest words from most to least difficult. Arrange the five simplest words from easier to easiest. Write a sentence describing why your hardest word was difficult to spell and why your easiest word was a snap.

6. Find as many smaller words as you can in each Blue Ribbon word. You may *not* mix up the letters in the word. For example, the word *example* contains four smaller words: *exam, ample, am,* and *amp.*

7. Write one synonym and one antonym for 15 Blue Ribbon words. Make a chart like this to show your work:

Blue Ribbon word	Synonym	Antonym

8. Write a poem using at least ten Blue Ribbon words. You may want to experiment with a particular poetry form, such as haiku or a cinquain.

9. Change ten Blue Ribbon words into new words by changing no more than three letters in each word. For example, the word *elated* can be changed to the word *flared* by changing the first **e** to **f** and the **t** to **r.** Making nouns plural, changing verb endings, or changing the total number of letters in a word is strictly prohibited.

10. Some of the Blue Ribbon words have several meanings. Research the words in the list and write down a new, unusual, or obscure meaning for at least ten of them. Use each word in a complete sentence that illustrates the unusual meaning you found.

Cutting It Short

1

General principle In a contraction, an apostrophe shows that one or several letters have been left out. Some words, however, become contracted or combined through use, and are recognized as new words without apostrophes.

Read the sentences below. Your Blue Ribbon words are underlined.

- The word <u>dumfound</u> was formed from the two words *dumb* and *confound.* (This word is sometimes spelled *dumbfound.*)
- *Splash* and *spatter* have been shortened to <u>splatter</u>.
- Do you know how we got the name of the meal we call <u>brunch</u>?
- The word <u>motorcade</u> is a combination of *cavalcade* and *motor cars.*
- <u>Melded</u> comes from the two words *melted* and *welded.*

1. Write your Blue Ribbon words on a sheet of paper.
2. Using a dictionary, write each word's phonetic spelling and definition. Then write each word in a new sentence.

3. Learn the spelling and definition of each Blue Ribbon word. Be prepared to write each word, properly spelled, in a complete sentence.

2

The Blue Ribbon words above are contractions of other words called *portmanteaus* (pôrt man' tōz). The author of *Alice In Wonderland,* Lewis Carroll, was famous for such portmanteaus as *snark* from *snake* and *shark,* and *slithy* from *slimy* and *lithe.*

Separate the portmanteaus below into their original words.

1. motel   _____ + _____
2. fishwich   _____ + _____
3. guesstimate   _____ + _____
4. smog   _____ + _____
5. fantabulous   _____ + _____

Make up some new portmanteaus from the following twosomes, or choose four of your own.

6. salt and pepper _____
7. cottage cheese _____
8. vinegar and oil _____
9. shoes and socks _____

3

Words that are commonly associated are sometimes collapsed together without contracting the two separate words. We call these new terms compound words. The space industry contributes many such new words. Use each of the compound terms below in a sentence.

1. moonport _____

2. spacewalk _____

3. lunarscape _____

4. payload _____

5. moonquake _____

6. liftoff _____

7. airlock _____

8. spacelab _____

9. crewmember _____

4

Contractions are sometimes confused with other words that sound the same but have completely different meanings. For example, *who's* and *whose*: "*Who's* responsible for this mess? *Whose* fault is it?"

Write a sentence for each contraction below and its homophone:

1. he'll, heel or heal _____

2. you're, your _____

3. we'd, weed _____

4. I'll, aisle _____

5. we've, weave _____

6. you'll, Yule _____

7. can't, cant _____

The Wild Wild West

1

General principle   When a word ends with a consonant plus **y,** we change the **y** to **i** before adding **-es** to make the word plural.

Read the paragraphs below. Your Blue Ribbon words are underlined.

"I have this all-fired great idea," drawled the sheriff of Drygulch County. "We ought to get us some <u>dromedaries</u> to ride on, out here in the deserts."

"I reckon that's not such a bad notion," agreed one of his <u>deputies</u>. "Especially since the infantry and the cavalry have <u>monopolies</u> on all the fast horses."

"Well then, it's agreed. You mosey on downtown and make a few <u>inquiries</u>," directed the sheriff. "With a stable full of camels, we can make these <u>territories</u> safe from outlaws once and for all!"

1. Write your Blue Ribbon words on a sheet of paper.
2. Using a dictionary, write each word's phonetic spelling and definition. Then write each word in a new sentence.
3. Learn the spelling and definition of each Blue Ribbon word. Be prepared to write each word, properly spelled, in a complete sentence.

2

Folks in the wild west had a vocabulary all their own, including each of the words below. Make these words part of your own vocabulary by using the *singular* form of each one in a sentence. Use your dictionary if necessary.

1. mesas
2. dogies
3. cowpokes
4. lassoes
5. pintos
6. posses
7. lariats
8. renegades
9. corrals
10. sentries

changing y to i   **63**

3

One night the sheriff and his deputies sat down to play a game of "Aces High."

"Here's how you play," instructed the sheriff. "I say a definition of a word which has the letters **a-c-e** in it, and you folks try to guess the word."

"That sure does sound like fun," groaned the deputies.

Here are the sheriff's clues. Fill in the answers.

1. Ties for shoes   __ a c e __

2. Movement with beauty   __ __ a c e

3. Ordinary   __ __ __ __ __ __ __ __ a c e

4. Walk anxiously back and forth   __ a c e

5. A running competition   __ a c e

6. Put back in position   __ __ __ __ a c e

7. Bring shame upon   __ __ __ __ __ a c e

8. How two computers work together   __ __ __ __ __ __ a c e

4

Cowboys and cowgirls are easily identified by their attire. The western-style hat in particular is associated with this occupation.

Each of the types of headgear below tells something about the person wearing it—or about the situation. Write one association for each article listed. Use your dictionary if necessary. The first one is done for you.

1. earmuffs _iceskaters_

2. helmet _____

3. bonnet _____

4. veil _____

5. beret _____

6. visor _____

7. top hat _____

8. hood _____

9. mortarboard _____

10. bandanna _____

Name three other pieces of headgear and identify a type of person who might wear each one—or when it would be worn.

11. _____

12. _____

13. _____

That's Using Your Head!

1

General principle   When we add **-ly** or **-ful** to a base word, we often change a final **y** to **i,** or sometimes drop a final **e.**

Read the paragraph below. Your Blue Ribbon words are underlined.

Being resourceful and <u>fanciful</u> are both important qualifications for becoming an inventor. <u>Bountiful</u> and original ideas are also a necessary part of the inventive process. The public can be <u>unmerciful</u> in criticizing new inventions. Most inventors themselves are <u>incredibly</u> critical of their own creations. Inventors are often <u>irretrievably</u> engrossed in their work, despite criticism from friends, family, and the public.

1. Write your Blue Ribbon words on a sheet of paper.
2. Using a dictionary, write each word's phonetic spelling and definition. Then write each word in a new sentence.
3. Learn the spelling and definition of each Blue Ribbon word. Be prepared to write each word, properly spelled, in a complete sentence.

2

Inventors are renowned for their sense of humor. In this activity, each inventor responds with a pun to the question, "How's your invention coming along?"

Example   The inventor of the alarm clock said loudly, "I'm running a bit late, but it's only a matter of time."

Write a "punny" response for each of the inventors below.

1. The inventor of the airplane said loftily, _____

_____

2. The inventor of the light bulb said brightly, _____

_____

3. The inventor of the computer said calculatingly, _____

_____

4. The inventor of handcuffs said captivatingly, _____

_____

5. The inventor of the iron said heatedly, _____

_____

6. The inventor of Popsicles said icily, _____

_____

3

These three real inventions were never big sellers, but they are fine examples of using your head. Each of these contraptions is patented. Write a brief paragraph describing what you think each one was intended to do.

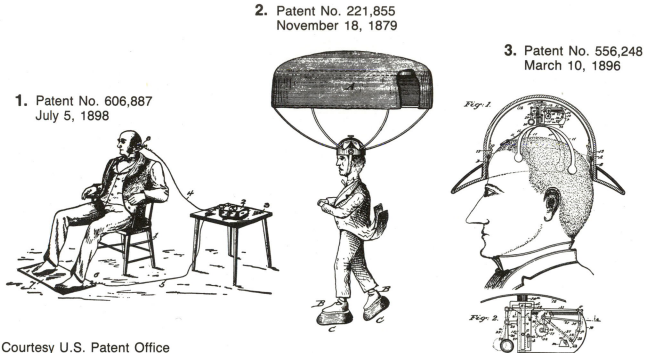

2. Patent No. 221,855
November 18, 1879

3. Patent No. 556,248
March 10, 1896

1. Patent No. 606,887
July 5, 1898

Courtesy U.S. Patent Office

4

Usually when the word *invention* is mentioned, people envision telephones, light bulbs, gasoline engines, and airplanes. Many important inventions, however, are not *things* and cannot be touched or seen. They are *processes,* or ways of doing things that develop gradually and make people's lives easier and more productive.

Which of the following process "inventions" do you feel has had the most beneficial impact on life today? Why? Write a paragraph stating your position. Remember, spelling counts!

1. Taking care of sick people in hospitals rather than at home.

2. Making things (such as cars) in pieces and putting them together on an assembly line, rather than making each item individually.

3. Having laws and courts to enforce laws rather than an "every-man-for-himself" society.

4. Providing schools for all children, regardless of their family's ability to pay.

A Statement of Fact

1

General principle   The names of these places of interest in the United States are as familiar to most people as the names of the states themselves. Notice that each of these sites is described by an open or closed compound word.

Read the sentences below. Your Blue Ribbon words are underlined.

- The 217-mile-long <u>Grand Canyon</u> is an immense gorge noted for its fantastic rock formations and its intense colors.
- Many earthquakes occur each year along the <u>San Andreas fault</u>.
- The <u>Everglades</u> are home to some of the most exotic wildlife in the United States.
- <u>Yellowstone</u> National Park is renowned for its geysers.
- <u>Niagara Falls</u> is a popular American honeymoon spot with an international border.

1. Write your Blue Ribbon words on a sheet of paper.
2. Using a dictionary, write each word's phonetic spelling and definition. Then write each word in a new sentence.
3. Learn the spelling and definition of each Blue Ribbon word. Be prepared to write each word, properly spelled, in a complete sentence.

2

Each Blue Ribbon word above names a natural wonder that's associated with a particular state. Write a complete sentence telling the location of each site and one interesting fact about it.

1. _____

_____

2. _____

_____

3. _____

_____

4. _____

_____

5. _____

_____

Each one of the United States has special crops and foods for which it is famous. See if you can associate a state with each food listed below. Remember, spelling counts!

1. maple syrup _____

2. peaches _____

3. baked potatoes _____

4. cheese _____

5. pralines _____

6. chili _____

7. lobsters _____

8. blueberries _____

9. apples _____

10. navel oranges _____

HINTS	
LA	ID
WA	GA
OR	TX
VT	ME
CA	WI

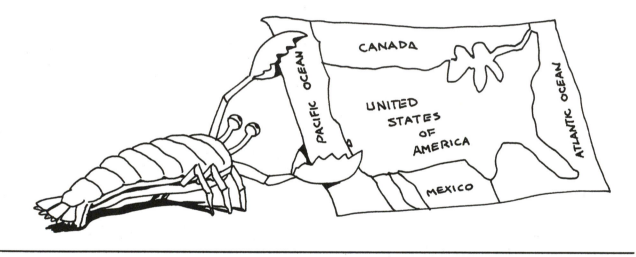

4

It is a statement of fact that the names of the states in each row below have something in common—phonetically speaking.

Write each state's full name and explain at least one common element. The first one is done for you.

1. TE, TX *Tennesee and Texas- both begin with T and have a short e sound.*

2. CA, CO, FL _____

3. MA, MS, MO _____

4. AL, AZ, OH _____

5. ID, OK, UT _____

6. AK, MN, PA, MT, NC _____

In My Estimation

1

General principle Adding the suffixes **-ion, -tion,** or **-ation** changes a verb into a noun. The spelling of the base word often changes when these suffixes are added.

Read the paragraph below. Your Blue Ribbon words are underlined.

   The thinking skill called <u>estimation</u> is very important in solving problems. When solving math problems, making an <u>approximation</u> before beginning to calculate can make the difference between success and failure. Giving <u>consideration</u> to the reasonableness of a final answer is also very important. One <u>option</u> for increasing your ability in this skill is to practice estimating in many different situations. While practice takes time, working on a problem without any idea of the answer can be pure <u>frustration</u>.

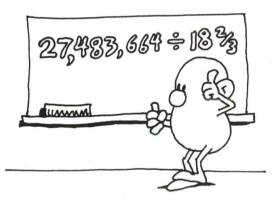

1. Write your Blue Ribbon words on a sheet of paper.
2. Using a dictionary, write each word's phonetic spelling and definition. Then write each word in a new sentence.
3. Learn the spelling and definition of each Blue Ribbon word. Be prepared to write each word, properly spelled, in a complete sentence.

2

Use the skill of estimation as you answer the questions below. Respond to each question with a complete sentence that contains the underlined word.

1. What is the average number of <u>exhalations</u> a fourth-grade child performs during each minute of a reading class?

   _____

2. What type of <u>vegetation</u> feeds most of the world's population?

   _____

3. What is the average number of days it takes to recover from a common cold <u>infection</u>?

   _____

4. What is the average body temperature of a ground squirrel or a bat in <u>hibernation</u>?

   _____

-ion, -tion, and -ation **69**

Many jobs require the ability to predict trends or patterns in people's tastes and behavior. Advertisers, for example, have to estimate what type of advertisement will sell a product to certain people.

Name at least five other occupations in which people must frequently predict the answers to questions. Describe a situation in each job when the skill would be used.

1. _____
   _____

2. _____
   _____

3. _____
   _____

4. _____
   _____

5. _____
   _____

4

Each of the words or phrases listed below is used in estimating measures and quantities. You must approximate the exact words, since all of the vowels are missing. Can you finish them so they are spelled exactly right?

1. __n th__ n___ghb__rh___d

2. __lm__st

3. n___rly

4. __ r___gh __st__m__t__

5. j__st __b___t

6. n___rl__

7. pr__ct__c__lly

8. __n th__ b__llp__rk

9. __ppr__x__m__t__ly

10. __n r___nd n__mb__rs

ESTIMATE THE NUMBER OF MARBLES IN THE JAR!! BEST GUESS WINS!! !! !! !! !! !! !! !!

-ion, -tion, and -ation

Blue Ribbon Review Lesson

Your Blue Ribbon Review Words

dumfound, splatter, brunch, motorcade, melded

dromedaries, deputies, monopolies, inquiries, directories

fanciful, bountiful, unmerciful, incredibly, irretrievably

Grand Canyon, San Andreas fault, Everglades, Yellowstone, Niagara Falls

estimation, approximation, consideration, option, frustration

Review Activities

Use your Blue Ribbon review words to complete as many of the following activities as your teacher assigns.

1. Classify all of the Blue Ribbon words into three separate categories, based on their phonetic respellings or their meanings. You may select *any three categories,* but every word on the list must fit into one of them.

2. Use at least 20 of the Blue Ribbon words in a short story of no longer than 300 words. You may use up to five Blue Ribbon words in the title.

3. Use a word search grid to create your own word search puzzle. Your puzzle should contain at least 15 Blue Ribbon words.

4. Arrange the Blue Ribbon words in "backwards" alphabetical order. In other words, first look at the *last* letter of each word to determine alphabetical order, then at the next-to-last letter, and so forth.

5. From the Blue Ribbon word lists, select the five easiest and the five hardest words to spell. Arrange the five hardest words from most to least difficult. Arrange the five simplest words from easier to easiest. Write a sentence describing why your hardest word was difficult to spell and why your easiest word was a snap.

6. Find as many smaller words as you can in each Blue Ribbon word. You may *not* mix up the letters in the word. For example, the word *example* contains four smaller words: *exam, ample, am,* and *amp.*

7. Write one synonym and one antonym for 15 Blue Ribbon words. Make a chart like this to show your work:

Blue Ribbon word	Synonym	Antonym

8. Write a poem using at least ten Blue Ribbon words. You may want to experiment with a particular poetry form, such as haiku or a cinquain.

9. Change ten Blue Ribbon words into new words by changing no more than three letters in each word. For example, the word *elated* can be changed to the word *flared* by changing the first **e** to **f** and the **t** to **r.** Making nouns plural, changing verb endings, or changing the total number of letters in a word is strictly prohibited.

10. Some of the Blue Ribbon words have several meanings. Research the words in the list and write down a new, unusual, or obscure meaning for at least ten of them. Use each word in a complete sentence that illustrates the unusual meaning you found.

Answer Key

Pages 1-2   Don't Be a Litterbug

Part 1

1. embankment (em bangk′ mənt)   a raised bank of earth or stones, used (in this case) to support a roadway.
2. malice (mal′ is)   ill will; a wish to hurt or make suffer.
3. candidly (can′ did lē)   frankly, sincerely.
4. habitat (hab′ ə tat)   place where someone lives; dwelling.
5. ample (am′ pəl)   more than enough.

Part 2

1. A scrăp of parchment: a bit of writing paper made from sheep- or goatskin.
2. a frăgment of insulation: a piece of material used to prevent heat transfer.
3. A plăstic receptacle: something of molded material used to contain smaller objects.
4. a pămphlet about ăsbĕstos: an unbound booklet about an insulating material.
5. a bĕnt spătula: a damaged, flat, thin tool used in the kitchen.

Part 3

1. tarăntula: a large hairy spider.
2. orăngutăn: a plant-eating, tree-dwelling ape.
3. stalked: hunted stealthily.
4. scăttering: throwing about; separating widely.
5. debris: remains of something broken or destroyed.
6. ĕnforcement: carrying out compelling rules.
7. agencies: businesses or establishments that work for others.
8. ăpprehĕnding: capturing and/or arresting.

Part 4

Answers will vary. Samples: bent, best, bet, every, lest, let, melt, met, nest, net, pelt, pen, pest, pet, rent, sense, sent, set, ten, tense, tent, test, upset, vest, yen.

Pages 3-4   The Hot Potato Test

Part 1

1. ponderous (pon′ dər əs)   large, heavy, burdensome.
2. intimated (in′ tə māt′ əd)   suggested, hinted.
3. responsibility (ri spon′ sə bil′ ə tē)   obligation, task.
4. disclose (dis klōz′)   uncover, make known, reveal.
5. illogical (i loj′ ə kəl)   not reasonable, foolish.

Part 2

Answers will vary.

Part 3

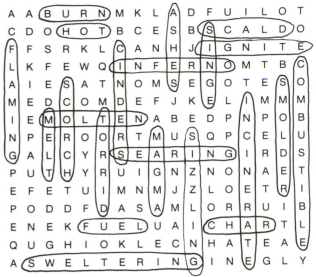

Part 4

"Children," Mr. Yellhizhedoff announced, "I want to see the tests you have devised. Stop the chatter immediately and let's get down to business. Benjamin, can you demonstrate your method to the class?"

"You bet!" answered Benjamin. He plopped a pat of butter on the top of the box.

"Good grief!" exclaimed Mr. Yellhizhedoff. "It's melting all over the lid!"

Pages 5-6   What's for Dinner?

Part 1

1. ingenious (in jē′ nyəs)   cleverly planned.
2. revitalized (rē vī′ tə līzd)   restored to vitality, given new life.
3. savory (sā′ vər ē)   pleasing in taste or smell.
4. elated (i lāt′ əd)   in high spirits, joyful.
5. belabor (bi lā′ bər)   work on to absurd lengths, with too much talk.

Part 2

1. Jams and Jellies   **2.** Seafood   **3.** Vegetables
4. Meats   **5.** Bakery Goods   **6.** Bakery Goods
7. Fruits   **8.** Vegetables   **9.** Herbs and Spices, or Vegetables (fresh)   **10.** Herbs and Spices, or Vegetables (fresh)   **11.** Meats   **12.** Seafood

Part 3

Answers will vary. Sample sentences:
1. He drained the water from cooked spaghetti.
2. He spread icing on a cake.
3. He spread juice over the chicken.
4. He made orange juice.
5. He served hot mustard with the green beans.
6. He used fresh parsley to decorate the chicken.
7. He made a salad.

Part 4

Take nine fresh apples and cut them into little pieces. Mix in some sugar and some flour and spices. Pour the mixture into a box of Ritz crackers. Shake it up. Empty the box into a pie pan. Bake in a 350° oven and serve it warm. It's delicious!

Pages 7-8   Meany Mouse Strikes Again

Part 1

1. notorious (nō tôr′ ē əs)   well-known for bad reasons, having a bad reputation.
2. atrocious (ə trō′ shəs)   monstrously wicked or cruel.
3. tyrant (tī′ rənt)   person who uses power cruelly or unjustly.
4. trifle (trī′ fəl)   treat someone without seriousness or respect.
5. odious (ō′ dē əs)   hateful, offensive.

Part 2

1. proceeded   **2.** fling   **3.** terrorized   **4.** bellowed
5. moldy   **6.** scurried   **7.** aggressor   **8.** cease

Part 3

Mīghty mīce unīte! Our hōme is gōing to be ōverrun. Gō hīde until the cōast is clear and the chīmes strīke fīve. Be as quīet as a mouse.
Total number /ō/: 5
Total number /ī/: 8

Part 4

1. catalog   **2.** catastrophe   **3.** catcher
4. caterpillar   **5.** catsup   **6.** cattle   **7.** catnap

---

Pages 9-10   Bored Silly

Part 1

1. dilemma (də lem′ ə)   a difficult situation.
2. hammock (ham′ ək)   a hanging bed, as of canvas, suspended by ropes.
3. haggling (hag′ ling)   arguing, disputing.
4. twiddle (twid′ l)   play with idly.
5. gibberish (jib′ ər ish)   senseless chatter, confused talk.

Part 2

1. hidden   **2.** summit   **3.** paddle   **4.** braggart
5. dimmer   **6.** beggar   **7.** madden   **8.** soggy
9. pebble   **10.** goggles

Part 3

Answers will vary. Sample:

m	d	b	g
mulling things over	driving across the desert	babysitting	getting a haircut
mopping floors	digging weeds	buttoning clothes	cutting the grass

---

Part 4

Answers will vary.

Pages 13-14   The Bermuda Triangle

Part 1

1. inroads (in′ rōdz)   advances, penetrations, incursions.
2. broached (brōcht)   began conversation or discussion about.
3. tainted (tānt′ əd)   stained, contaminated.
4. disarray (dis′ ə rā′)   disorder, confusion.
5. foreshadowed (fôr shad′ ōd)   warned of, indicated beforehand.

Part 2

The doomed vessels are those with the words **staid, reproach, coax, relay,** and **hallow.**

Part 3

Answers will vary. Samples:
1. Maybe more ships than planes pass through the Bermuda Triangle, so it just looks as if the area is more dangerous for ships.
2. The premise doesn't give us any figures on how many ships and planes disappear *outside* the triangle, so we can't assume that it's safer outside.
3. Maybe no hot-air balloon has ever passed through the triangle; we don't know because the premise doesn't mention hot-air balloons at all.

Part 4

My days are filled with the fellowship of sailors and the spray of waves lapping against the bow. The remains of boats that have strayed too close to the Bermuda Triangle float slowly by. I will praise the day we are through these straits and the coast of America is in sight.

Pages 15-16   Substitutes

Part 1

1. careened (kə rēnd′)   swayed sharply, leaned to one side.
2. seethe (sēth)   be excited, be disturbed.
3. deem (dēm)   think, believe, or consider.
4. appease (ə pēz′)   pacify, calm or quiet a disturbed person.
5. breach (brēch)   break, neglect, infraction.

Part 2

"What's going on!" the principal screeched when she heard the clamor coming from Room 4. "Heed my words," she announced as she entered the noisy classroom. "I become quite peevish when I see a class with this kind of demeanor. I do not consider your feats to be appropriate school behavior. I think you are all in league against your substitute, Mrs. Whymee. We will have no further dealings on this matter. Is that clear?"

Part 3

Team I—/e/: death, heavy, pleasant, wealthy, pheasant, sweat, dealt, healthy, leaden, realm

Team II—/ē/: cheap, lease, plea, defeat, yeast, preach, creak, steam, reteach, meager

Part 4

Answers will vary. Samples: answered, bellowed, called, declared, emphasized, fretted, gasped, heckled, implored, joked, kidded, laughed, mocked, noted, ordered, pleaded, questioned, responded, stated, tattled, urged, vowed, whispered, yelled.

Pages 17-18 Never Cry Wolf

Part 1

1. infantile (in' fən tīl) childish.
2. remote (ri mōt') distant, slight, faint.
3. precise (pri sīs') exact, accurate.
4. agitate (aj' ə tāt) disturb, excite.
5. chastise (cha' stīz) punish.

Part 2

Answers will vary.

Part 3

1. to run away.
2. to make ready for action.
3. to become suddenly and unreasonably afraid.
4. to run away in panic (usually a group).
5. to move suddenly or nervously.
6. to give up for the sake of something.
7. to contribute to a good cause.
8. to react favorably.
9. to refuse to take notice.
10. to stare openmouthed.

Part 4

Answers will vary.

Pages 19-20 Sound Off

Part 1

1. knoll (nōl) a small, rounded hill.
2. numbing (num' ing) dulling the feelings (as with cold).
3. wringing (ring' ing) so wet that liquid can be squeezed out.
4. knapsacks (nap' saks) canvas bags for carrying things on the back.
5. gnarled (närld) knotted, twisted.

Part 2

Answers will vary.

Part 3

Answers will vary. Samples:

Consonant Blends: ping, swish, plop, crackle, screech, click

Stressed Consonant: fizz, sizzle, whiz, whir, purr, hiss

Repeated Sound or Syllable: ding dong, splish splash, tick tock, beep beep, pitter patter, rat a tat tat

Part 4

Answers will vary. Samples:

1. The ocean *roared* at the sailors.
2. The pines *whispered* near the tent.
3. The brook *babbled* to the picnickers.
4. The old gate *complained* as it swung open.
5. The kettle *whistled cheerfully* on the stove.
6. The wind *howled* in my ears.
7. The foghorn *called mournfully* to the ships.
8. The rain *pounded angrily* on the roof.

Pages 21-22 Bumper Stickers

Part 1

1. skeptical (skep' tə kəl) inclined to doubt; not believing.
2. snags (snagz) unexpected obstacles.
3. smudged (smujd) smeared; marked with dirty streaks.
4. postponed (pōst pōnd') delayed; put off till a later time.
5. obstacle (ob' stə kəl) something that stands in the way or stops progress.

Part 2

Answers will vary.

Part 3 and Part 4

Answers will vary.

Pages 25-26 Water, Water, Everywhere

Part 1

1. lieutenant (lü ten' ənt) a police department officer.
2. sediment (sed' ə mənt) matter that settles to the bottom of a liquid.
3. iridescent (ir' ə des' ənt) displaying changing colors.
4. silt (silt) fine particles of earth carried by moving water.
5. asphalt (as' fôlt) a mixture used to pave streets.

Part 2

Answers will vary.

Part 3

The torrent of water pushed the fragile life raft into the swift current. Looking behind her, Carmen saw that the aft section of the ship was still visible, tilted upward. Looking back was too difficult. She turned away and gathered her puppy Somersault into the remnant of a quilt that she had. Only a soft tuft of fur was visible as the puppy shifted his body closer for warmth. They were adrift on the vast, vacant ocean.

Part 4

1. an ant chant   2. a spent cent   3. faint paint
4. a pliant giant   5. a pleasant pheasant
6-8. Answers will vary.

Pages 27-28   A Matter of Taste

Part 1

1. comical (kom′ ə kəl)   amusing, funny.
2. contemplating (kon′ təm plā′ ting)   thinking carefully about.
3. broccoli (brok′ l ō)   a green vegetable with stems and flower heads.
4. currant (kẻr′ ənt)   a very small, seedless raisin.
5. maverick (mav′ ər ik)   a person who refuses to go along with the norm.

Part 2

Answers will vary. All the words should be circled EXCEPT **luscious, spicy,** and **chewy.**

Part 3

Food: maize, kale, okra, artichoke, kohlrabi, chard, coriander, leek, scallion, lentil.
Utensils: sieve, colander, casserole, spatula, crock, corer, ricer, pestle, whisk, cleaver.

Part 4

Laura ordered the egg grinder. Mom ordered broiled hamburger. Gramps ordered salad. Patrick ordered fried fish.

Pages 29-30   Believe It or Not

Part 1

1. endowed (en doud′)   having an inborn ability or talent.
2. trouncing (troun′ sing)   a beating, defeat.
3. towering (tou′ ər ing)   very great.
4. astounded (ə stoun′ dəd)   shocked with amazement or surprise.
5. oust (oust)   forced out, driven out.

Part 2

I found the crown on the ground near the flower garden behind the house. The crooks are prowling about the town. Pounce on them and impound them now!

Part 3

Answers will vary. Samples: **1.** quick as a microchip **2.** white as an iceberg **3.** light as popped corn **4.** mad as a racer with a flat tire **5.** easy as breathing **6.** slow as a flowering bud **7.** straight as a ruler **8.** sharp as a laser beam **9.** neat as a hospital bed **10.** hard as a skull

Part 4

1. Show does not belong because **ow** is pronounced /ō/.
2. Aglow does not belong because **ow** is pronounced /ō/.
3. Though does not belong because **ou** is pronounced /ō/.
4. Uncouth does not belong because **ou** is pronounced /ū/.

Pages 31-32   Out of This World

Part 1

1. confirmed (kən fẻrmd′)   gave assurance of the truth of something.
2. terminal (tẻr′ mə nəl)   station for a vehicle.
3. authorized (ô′ thə rīzd)   gave the power or authority to.
4. hurtled (hẻr′ tld)   rushed violently.
5. solar (sō′ lər)   related to the sun.

Part 2

Our instruments show a solar disturbance. The ship crossed through a meteor shower. Yesterday Surveyor was damaged in a crater on the lunar surface. We are experiencing turbulence now. We are approaching the outer boundary of Jupiter. Over and out.

Part 3

1. anteater 2. turtle 3. sea urchin 4. termites
5. rhinoceros 6. giraffe 7. lizard

Part 4

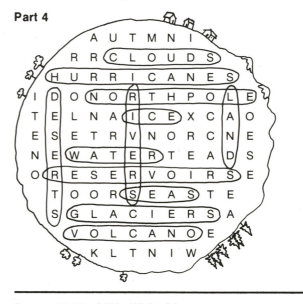

Pages 33-34   Little White Lies

Part 1

1. gaudy (gô′ dē)   cheap and showy.
2. flawless (flô′ lis)   without fault; perfect.
3. fraud (frôd)   a dishonest person.
4. plausible (plô′ zə bəl)   believable.
5. scrawl (skrôl)   poor, careless handwriting.

Part 2

1. authentic, being what it seems to be 2. true to life, genuine 3. frank, marked by honesty
4. truthful 5. characterized by falsehood, deceit
6. straightforward 7. not true 8. absolutely and completely true 9. not reliable, deceitful
10. crafty, sneaky

Part 3

1. F 2. F 3. F 4. F 5. F 6. T 7. F 8. F
9. T 10. F

Part 4

Answers will vary. Samples:

1. Once you have told a lie, it will never go away; the harm it did will remain forever.

2. If you ignore a lie, it can't harm you for long, but will disappear over time.

Pages 37-38   Don't Bug Me

Part 1

1. swallowtail (swol′ ō tāl)   large butterfly with tail-like extensions of hind wings.

2. dragonfly (drag′ ən flī)   insect with long body and two pairs of gauzy wings.

3. silverfish (sil′ vər fish′)   small wingless insects with silvery scales.

4. praying mantis (prā′ ing man′ tis)   insect that captures others with its long forelegs.

5. cockroach (cok′ rōch)   brown, nocturnal insect; common household pest.

Part 2

Answers will vary. Samples: butterfly, horsefly, mayfly, fruit fly, deer fly, firefly, ladybug, sow bug, June bug, lightning bug, leafhopper, ant lion, inchworm, water strider, lacewing, glowworm, bumblebee, honeybee, yellow jacket, gypsy moth, black widow, trapdoor spider, housefly, grasshopper, boll weevil, corn ear worm, Japanese beetle, potato beetle, mealworm, stinkbug.

Part 3

Answers will vary.

Part 4

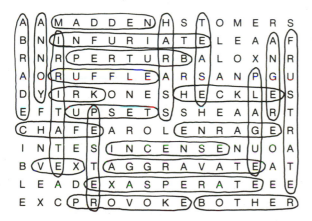

Pages 39-40   Happy Holidays

Part 1

1. Memorial Day (mə môr′ ē əl dā)   honoring American servicemen who have died.

2. Admission Day (ad mish′ ən dā)   the day a state was admitted to the union.

3. Independence Day (in′ di pen′ dəns dā) celebrating a country's freedom from a colonial power.

4. Mardi Gras (mär′ dē grä)   Shrove Tuesday, the last day before Lent.

5. Arbor Day (är bər dā)   day set aside for the planting of trees.

Part 2

Answers will vary.

Part 3

Answers will vary. Sample sentences:

1. Pyrotechnics are fireworks set off on the Fourth of July.

2. A cornucopia, or horn of plenty, is filled with fruits, vegetables, and nuts at Thanksgiving.

3. A menorah is a candlestick with eight branches used in Jewish homes during Chanukah.

4. A nosegay is a colorful bouquet given on holidays such as Valentine's Day, May Day, or Mother's Day.

5. Confetti are small bits of paper tossed into the air on New Year's Eve to celebrate the start of a new year.

6. A crèche is the nativity scene, often seen in Christian homes at Christmas.

7. Masquerades are costumes with masks worn at Halloween or during Mardi Gras.

8. A piñata is a paper-covered pot filled with candy and presents, popular during the Christmas season.

9. A ballot is the paper or card that people use on Election Day to cast their votes.

10. A specter is a terrifying ghost seen by those with vivid imaginations on Halloween (also by Scrooge in Dickens's *A Christmas Carol*).

Part 4

Answers will vary. Samples: party goods stores, toy stores, firecracker manufacturers, florists, airlines, jewelers, candlemakers, Christmas tree farms, turkey farms, pumpkin farms, ski resorts, greeting card companies, costume stores.

Pages 41-42   Mind Your Manners

Part 1

1. imprudent (im prüd′ ənt)   rash, unwise.

2. unreasonable (un rē′ zn ə bəl)   excessive, asking too much.

3. immaturity (im′ ə chür′ ə tē)   young, undeveloped, babyish way.

4. irresponsible (ir i spon′ sə bəl)   untrustworthy, unreliable.

5. inconsiderate (in kən sid′ ər it)   not thoughtful of others and their feelings.

Part 2

1. immodest   **2.** unfeeling   **3.** undamaged
4. uncanny   **5.** infirm   **6.** unforgettable
7. unequaled   **8.** impolite   **9.** impure

Part 3

Answers will vary.

Part 4

Answers may vary. Samples: **1.** shirt **2.** an artist **3.** a tablecloth **4.** a thermometer **5-6.** Answers will vary.

Pages 43-44   What's So Funny?

Part 1

1. jovial (jō′ vē əl)   good-humored and merry.
2. obliged (ə blījd′)   forced, duty-bound.
3. majority (mə jôr′ ə tē)   the largest number; more than half.
4. indulge (in dulj′)   give in to the wishes of someone; humor someone.
5. generate (jen′ ə rāt)   produce; come up with.

Part 2

1. **gouged** should be **gorged.**
2. **beagle** should be **bagel.**
3. **epidemic** should be **hypodermic.**
4. **fun** should be **fund.**
5. **Umpire** should be **Empire.**
6. **camellia** should be **chameleon.**

Part 3

Answers will vary.

Part 4

Answers will vary. Samples:
1. "E=mc², " Einstein cried energetically.
2. "I'll try a spice cookie," she said gingerly.
3. "Don't lean on the tent poles!" he said rigidly.
4. "He's with the FBI," she observed intelligently.
5. "When will you marry me?" he asked engagingly.

Pages 45-46   Going, Going, Gone

Part 1

1. platypuses (plat′ ə pús əz)   egg-laying mammals.
2. nautiluses (nô′ tl əs əz)   pearly, multi-chambered mollusks.
3. oryxes (ôr′ iks əz)   large gray African antelope with long, straight horns.
4. carcasses (kär′ kəs əz)   bodies of dead animals.
5. bulrushes (búl′ rush əz)   tall, slender grasses that grow in or near water.

Part 2

1. sloth **2.** clowder **3.** skulk **4.** herd **5.** rafter **6.** colony **7.** flock **8.** gaggle **9.** litter **10.** troop **11.** swarm **12.** pack **13.** pride **14.** pod **15.** bevy

Part 3

1. knee pants
2. young girls in the roaring twenties
3. gathered material that puffed up at the back of skirts
4. tools that pulled tiny shoe buttons through the buttonholes or loops
5. hair-slicking greases

6. writing instruments
7. glasses composed of a single round glass for one eye
8. people in the 50's and early 60's who rejected conventional society
9. frilly umbrellas designed to keep off the sun
10. old-fashioned record players
11-14. Answers will vary.

Part 4

Answers will vary.

Pages 49-50   Just Desserts

Part 1

1. ravenous (rav′ ə nəs)   very hungry.
2. suet (sü′ it)   a kind of hard fat from cattle and sheep.
3. cinnamon (sin′ ə mən)   spice made from the dried bark of the laurel tree.
4. crescent (kres′ nt)   a curved shape like the quarter moon.
5. luscious (lush′ əs)   richly sweet; delicious.

Part 2 and Part 3

Answers will vary.

Part 4

Dearest Family: I am leaving an exceptionally delicious chocolate cake on the counter for your dessert. Do not consume this cake before supper. I insist that you finish every morsel of casserole before you slice a piece. You may have milk or cider with the cake—absolutely no soda tonight! Disregarding my orders will result in a suspension of privileges. I am serious! Your loving mother. P.S. Brush and floss your teeth before bed!

Pages 51-52   Double Play

Part 1

1. crammed (kramd)   crowded; filled to the limit.
2. donned (dond)   put on.
3. dubbed (dubd)   nicknamed; called.
4. banning (ban′ ing)   prohibit from taking part in.
5. trekked (trekt)   traveled slowly.

Part 2

"Double" words: twofold, Twins, paired, double-header, half, second, bifocals, twice, couple, duplicate
Double-consonant words: stunning, runners, winning (Note that **inning** and **missed,** while they have double consonants, do not follow the general principle.)

Part 3

Answers will vary. Sample word twins: down and out, short but sweet, hale and hearty, pick and choose, salt and pepper.

Part 4

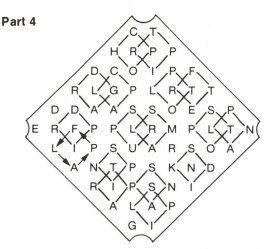

Past tense forms: flapped, chopped, clapped, dripped, dragged, fretted, planned, plotted, skidded, slammed, slipped, snipped, spanned, spotted, spurred, trapped, tripped.

Pages 53-54   Little by Little

Part 1

1. dwindling (dwind' ling)   becoming smaller and smaller; shrinking.
2. decreasing (di krēs' ing)   growing less in supply.
3. belittled (bi lit' ld)   made to seem unimportant.
4. reducing (ri düs' ing)   lowering; making less in amount.
5. abated (ə bāt' əd)   reduced, decreased.

Part 2 and Part 3

Answers will vary.

Part 4

Answers may vary. Samples: ail, all, an, ant, aunt, in, input, it, lap, lint, lip, lull, nail, nap, pail, pal, pall, pan, pant, pill, pit, plant, pliant, punt, put, tail, tall, tan, tap, till, tip, up.

Pages 55-56   Better Sopper-Uppers

Part 1

1. heftiest (hef' tē əst)   most substantial; strongest.
2. soggier (sog' ē ər)   wetter, more soaked.
3. grimier (grī' mē ər)   dirtier.
4. ornerier (ôrn' rē ər)   meaner.
5. thriftiest (thrif' tē əst)   most economical; with the most savings.

Part 2

Answers will vary. Sample sentences:

1. Caulking fills cracks, as in a boat, that seep water.
2. Dehumidifiers remove moisture from the air.
3. Sandbags are placed along stream and river banks to prevent flooding.
4. Gauze compresses absorb blood and fluids from wounds.
5. Dikes are built on river banks to contain the water and prevent overflowing.
6. Cornstarch absorbs water in cooking.

Sample substances: sponges, napkins, paper towels, towels, shower curtains, raincoats, umbrellas, sweatbands, gutters, kitty litter, diapers, nose plugs.

Part 3

1. protest   2. modest   3. suggest   4. request
5. honest   6. jest   7. harvest   8. contest   9. detest
10. digest

Part 4

Answers will vary. Samples: 1. cleaner than a bar of soap   2. stronger than a steel cable   3. skinnier than a strand of spaghetti   4. smoother than a new-varnished desk top   5. flatter than a piece of stepped-on gum   6. stiffer than a new shoe
7. happier than a cat in a catnip patch

Pages 57-58   Same But Different

Part 1

1. corps (kôr)   a military unit, smaller than an army.
2. mustered (mus' tərd)   gathered together, collected.
3. symbol (sim' bəl)   something that stands for an idea.
4. roll (rōl)   rapid, continuous beating.
5. soared (sôrd)   rose to great heights.

Part 2

Answers will vary. The homophones are **core, mustard, cymbal, role,** and **sword.**

Part 3

Answers will vary. The dual meanings are:

1. sow—to plant; sow—a pig.
2. tear—to rip; tear—a salty drop from the eye.
3. wind—to twist or turn; wind—moving air.
4. desert—to leave; desert—hot sandy place.
5. record—to put in permanent form; record—a disc with sound on it.
6. close—to shut; close—near.

Part 4

My dear family, I have missed you these many days. As I rest here writing to you, I hear the peal of thunder and see the flare of lightning. The road is filled with currents of rain water. Our horses sink in the mud and neigh in pain. Two boys died yesterday. At times I lose heart and I wonder if I am a coward. I wish this war would end. Your son, Sol

---

Pages 61-62   Cutting It Short

Part 1

1. dumfound (dum' found)   amaze, bewilder, confuse.
2. splatter (splat' ər)   cause liquid to spray about in scattered drops.
3. brunch (brunch)   a morning meal between breakfast and lunch.
4. motorcade (mō' tər kād)   a long line or parade of cars.
5. melded (meld' əd)   to blend, merge, unite.

Part 2

1. motor + hotel **2.** fish + sandwich **3.** guess + estimate **4.** smoke + fog **5.** fantastic + fabulous
6-9. Answers will vary.

Part 3 and Part 4

Answers will vary.

Pages 63-64 The Wild Wild West

Part 1

1. dromedaries (drom' ə der' ēz) one-humped camels.
2. deputies (dep' yə tēz) persons appointed as assistants to the sheriff.
3. monopolies (mə nop' ə lēz) exclusive control of something.
4. inquiries (in kwī' rēz) searches for information.
5. directories (də rek' tər ēz) book listing names and addresses.

Part 2

Answers will vary. Singular forms are: **1.** mesa
2. dogie or dogy **3.** cowpoke **4.** lasso **5.** pinto
6. posse **7.** lariat **8.** renegade **9.** corral
10. sentry

Part 3

1. laces **2.** grace **3.** commonplace **4.** pace
5. race **6.** replace **7.** disgrace **8.** interface

Part 4

Answers will vary. Samples: **1.** iceskater **2.** football player **3.** baby **4.** bride **5.** artist **6.** golfer
7. groom **8.** monk **9.** graduate **10.** gypsy
11-13. Answers will vary.

Pages 65-66 That's Using Your Head!

Part 1

1. fanciful (fan' sə fəl) imaginative.
2. bountiful (boun' tə fəl) plentiful, abundant.
3. unmerciful (un mėr' si fəl) cruel, without mercy.
4. incredibly (in kred' ə blē) unbelievably.
5. irretrievably (ir' i trē' və blē) unable to be recalled or restored; as if lost.

Part 2

Answers will vary. Samples:
1. "Things are looking up!"
2. "I can see the light at the end of the tunnel."
3. "It's a total success."
4. "I have it all locked up now!"
5. "I still have a few wrinkles to smooth out."
6. "I almost have the problem licked."

Part 3

Answers will vary. The *real* intent of these patented items was as follows:
1. This invention was a machine purportedly for the electric extraction of poisons.

2. This invention was one man's idea of a fire escape.
3. This contraption is a self-tipping hat; it could be tipped upon meeting someone, to show one's respect.

Part 4

Answers will vary.

Pages 67-68 A Statement of Fact

Part 1

1. Grand Canyon (grand can' yən) gorge of the Colorado River, in Arizona.
2. San Andreas fault (san an drā' əs fôlt) an earthquake zone in California.
3. Everglades (ev' ər glādz) a large swamp in Florida.
4. Yellowstone (yel' ō stōn) a large park in Wyoming.
5. Niagara Falls (nī ag' rə fôlz) waterfall between the U.S. (New York) and Canada.

Part 2

Answers will vary.

Part 3

1. Vermont **2.** Georgia **3.** Idaho **4.** Wisconsin
5. Louisiana **6.** Texas **7.** Maine **8.** Oregon
9. Washington **10.** California

Part 4

1. Texas and Tennessee; both begin with **t** and have the /e/ sound.
2. California, Colorado, and Florida; they all have the /or/ sound.
3. Massachusetts, Mississippi, and Missouri; they all have a double **s**.
4. Alabama, Arizona, and Ohio; each one begins and ends with the same letter.
5. Idaho, Oklahoma, and Utah; each begins with a long vowel.
6. Alaska, Minnesota, Pennsylvania, Montana, and North Carolina; they all end with the letter **a**.

Pages 69-70 In My Estimation

Part 1

1. estimation (es tə mā' shən) judging the approximate value or amount.
2. approxmation (ə prok' sə mā' shən) a nearly correct amount, not exact.
3. consideration (kən sid' ə rā' shən) attention, thought.
4. option (op' shən) choice, alternative.
5. frustration (fru strā' shən) being thwarted, baffled.

Part 2

1. 35 exhalations **2.** rice **3.** 7-10 days **4.** about 32.5 degrees (just above freezing)

Part 3

Answers will vary. Samples:

1. Economists predict the effects of political events on the economy.

2. Weather forecasters predict the path of a hurricane.

3. Research scientists predict the results of their experiments.

4. Sports coaches predict what the opposing team will do.

5. Book publishers predict how many copies of a new book will sell.

Part 4

1. in the neighborhood. **2.** almost **3.** nearly **4.** a rough estimate **5.** just about **6.** nearly

7. practically **8.** in the ballpark **9.** approximately

10. in round numbers